MASTER
THE ART OF
LEARNING

A PRACTICAL GUIDE TO *HIGH PERFORMANCE MEMORY SKILLS* TO ADVANCE YOUR CAREER

PETER SZCZENSNY

Cover design by 100Covers.com
Interior design by formattedbooks.com

ISBN (print):   978-3-949279-00-3
ISBN (eBook):   978-3-949279-01-0

GET YOUR FREE RESOURCES TODAY!

As a way of thanking you for buying my book, I would like to offer you a few additional FREE resources that will help you implement the techniques I teach you in this book.

Just go to

masteroflearning.com

and you will get instant access!

TABLE OF CONTENTS

FOREWORD

In today's fast-moving age, many of us are overwhelmed by the flood of information we receive on a daily basis. For this very reason, the ability to memorise and recall information is becoming the most important factor in distinguishing the successful from the unsuccessful, the winners from the losers, the haves from the have-nots. This applies even more to the professional arena, where those who continuously work at developing their skills, gaining new knowledge and preparing for new challenges are more likely to be ready when opportunity strikes. When you have the skills and knowledge you need for your next step and also the confidence that you can learn anything new quickly, you are far more likely to get the promotion you have been working toward or find that new job that rewards you with new skills and abilities.

Due to the COVID-19 crisis, the world is in a state of economic turbulence as unemployment numbers increase across the globe. The US and the UK are being hit particularly hard. Anyone losing their job during these troublesome times is facing an even tougher job market than before, so having something that distinguishes you from others is even more important than ever. Outstanding learning skills could be the one factor that sets you apart and helps you find a new job—maybe even a way better job than the one you've had so far. Knowing proven memory techniques that have been around for over 2,500 years can help you achieve this.

Most of us have never learnt *how* to learn—or even how to study. In schools around the world, teachers present pupils with materials that the pupils then have to memorise somehow using simple memorisation aids such as acronyms, rhymes and catchy sentences. These tactics, however, do not actually inspire pupils, so as adults they are not too eager to learn and study either. You cannot expect an uninspired person to advance their professional skills without knowing how to *actually* retain information.

While the memory techniques I have mentioned above will require an initial time investment to learn and practise, they will pay huge dividends both in terms of better results and significant time savings for anyone who applies them. From my own experience, I have seen that the main challenge to professional learning is time. Many of us spend more than an hour commuting to and from work every day. By the time we get home in the evening we are tired, exhausted and the last thing on our minds is sitting down and studying. We would rather spend the time we have left in the day with the loved ones who are happy to see us when we get home. Despite life's responsibilities—household chores or helping the children with their homework—with just a little bit of effort, you *can* reap the benefits of these specific techniques.

Whether it is names, numbers, vocabulary, mathematical formulas or lists of facts, you can apply the memory techniques in this book to these areas and many others. I will show you how to do this with practical examples so that when you start a new learning project you can apply these methods yourself. I have had the privilege of introducing hundreds of people to these memory techniques so far—pupils, students and professionals (particularly salespeople). The positive feedback from those who have applied these techniques is a continuing motivation for me to spread the use of these techniques to as many people as possible.

I was fortunate to have grown up in a household where we would often sit together long after our Sunday lunches and listen to my father explain the world to us. He would explain how various machines worked, events in history, all the interesting things we had observed or heard about during the week of which we were eager to understand the inner workings. It bound us together as a family and made gaining knowledge something that I remember with fondness. This has given me a very positive view on learning.

Learning languages has been a keen interest of mine since my school days, and I kept this up even after my formal education was over. Little did I know that I could have saved much of the time I spent learning foreign words and their meaning and grammatical structure had I known the techniques and approaches that I will introduce to you in this book. It was only after ten years of working as a professional that I had the good fortune of attending a one-day course on memory techniques and the even greater luck of being able to take a vacation soon afterwards. I took one of the recommended books on memory techniques with me and worked through it during the extent of the trip.

It was quite an exciting learning journey (on top of the fantastic time I had exploring New Zealand and Fiji!). Along the way I discovered how powerful the combination of motivation, focus and the right techniques could be in studying and learning new things. Names, numbers, lists of facts - these suddenly stuck in my memory much more easily, faster and for a longer time, not to mention that it was far more fun this way!

I often get asked, "Peter, if I have always had good grades in school and at university, can I still benefit from your course?" The answer is a clear yes! Even somebody who is already successful at school, university or at work can still reduce the time and effort spent learning new materials by applying these techniques. So even if you get nothing else out of this book, just learning how to save time will be of significant benefit to you.

One participant from a workshop, Alexandra, wrote to me afterwards telling me how happy she was with what she had learnt. There was one thing in particular that she said made her everyday life easier. She wrote, "When I go jogging and think about my job, now I have a simple way to remember all my good ideas without having to write them down. This has helped me become much more productive than before."

Another participant, Olaf, a salesman, spends a great deal of his day in the car often listening to audiobooks on professional development topics such as selling skills. Before taking part in my course, he would only remember very little of the specifics, so if he really wanted to apply some of the recommended selling techniques, he would have to listen to the audiobooks multiple times. Now he can remember far more of the recommendations the first time around since he has learnt how to take mental notes. This he can do easily while driving and his sales have already started to improve.

Another very satisfying form of feedback I receive is when I teach children how to learn the vocabulary of a foreign language. Once they start having fun creating their little memory pictures and stories to remember the words and their meaning and spelling, their eyes light up because they know they will never have to work hard again to remember these words. Often, they cannot stop telling everyone around them what they have just achieved! With these techniques, learning literally becomes child's play!

When you look at the incredible challenges that participants in memory championships have been able to conquer, such as learning over two hundred random numbers in five minutes or the faces and names of over one hundred people in fifteen minutes, it gives you a good idea of what is possible using the techniques in this book. Our goal here is not to perform similar feats (although you could with sufficient practice!) but to be able to learn more quickly and easily for the long term. The basic techniques are still the same for both and are as powerful for you and me as they are for the memory champions. You can reduce the time it takes to learn and store information by just adding a few strategies that make it possible for you to transfer anything you have learnt into your long-term memory.

I am often asked what kind of memory improvements are possible. The answer depends on factors such as the strategies you already use and how much you will practise these techniques, among others. My minimal expectation—as should be yours—is that you double your learning speed with ease by applying what you learn in this book and doing the exercises. I had to go down the same path you will take and along the way I have created a few support tools that have made it very easy for me to practise these techniques. Since I want you to succeed in developing your learning skills, I am making these tools available to you for free.

I have read that many people put down a book after reading the first chapter. From my own experience, I know that that can happen quite easily. Sometimes, I pick up a book and it looks interesting, but then life happens, different tasks require my attention and before I know it, I have forgotten about the book. Please do not fall into this trap. If you do, you will miss out on the proven strategies that people across the centuries have used to learn more quickly, more easily, and for the long term. The longer you wait, the longer it will take you to know how to save time learning and achieving greater success.

To help you along your journey, I would like to invite you to join my email reminder service. These reminders serve as subtle nudges so you remember to take the next step along the way. They will encourage you to not miss out on the great potential of developing your memory—and with that, the possibilities in life. Just go to www.masteroflearning.com to sign up and have access to all the resources I mention in this book, all for free.

Let's dive into the first section where I will tell you more about me and the memory techniques that will change your memory and—when you apply them correctly—also your life! Enjoy the journey, be open and playful and see you in the first chapter.

CHAPTER 1

INTRODUCTION

My own learning journey

When I need to learn something nowadays, my approach to learning is different from how I learned at school or even at university. Back then I had heard about mnemonic devices that made learning some things easier, like the order of the major keys or the guitar strings, and in history there were some funny sayings to remember the dates of a few historical events, but there was not much beyond that. What I had already deduced for myself was that it was easier to learn something if I created shortcuts that somehow reminded me of that thing.

But it was not a systematic approach. I didn't really have a structured plan, and often enough I had to use rote learning, pushing content into my brain through brute force repetition. When I was fifteen, I bought my first memory course. I was fascinated by the idea that there could be different approaches to learning that would make it easier and faster for me to learn, store and recall information. Unfortunately, the course was written in rather lengthy and tedious language, so I did not get very far—but at least my interest was piqued.

My school and university days were nonetheless quite successful. In retrospect, I understand some of the things that helped me to learn, but some things could have been much easier. I still remember clearly how I walked through the streets of Oxford before my final exams at university after some very intensive learning sessions. I tried to avoid any contact with other people because I was afraid that my laboriously acquired knowledge would suddenly vanish if I stopped concentrating on it even for a moment. It seemed to me as if I would have to carry a big bowl filled up to the top with water through the city and I had to be very careful that the water, which was sloshing back and forth in the bowl, did not run out. This shows how unsure I felt about what I had memorised for my exam preparations. As you can imagine, the information didn't stay in my memory past the exams!

Twelve years ago, I finally got the chance to attend a seminar that introduced me to the wonderful world of memory techniques. Here I learned how to memorise numbers, names and faces, lists of facts (even the most abstract ones), among other things in a simple and structured way. Since then, I have been fascinated by how much easier learning has become *just because* I use a few simple techniques. Today, when I call colleagues or friends, I often dial their numbers from memory so I don't have to look them up in my contacts. Or when I'm travelling by train, which happened regularly pre–COVID-19, even on journeys with two or three changes of trains I can easily remember when I leave and where, on which platform and in which car I have reserved which seat. You may object that this may not seem useful, but I always feel it is a nice little triumph when I know I don't have to dig out my mobile phone and look up these details; it is at least a small contribution to making my travel more relaxed.

I have been using these techniques for quite a few years now. I have taught many colleagues, other professionals and also children, teenagers and students. And although they are up to 2,500 years old (the techniques, not the colleagues) and dating back to the time of the ancient Greeks and Romans, they have proven to be very effective. Since those ancient times, however, they have naturally developed further and can be applied specifically to the requirements of our modern times. I will show you exactly how in this book.

Why I have written this book

When I started to apply memory techniques more intensively twelve years ago, it was initially out of pure curiosity. In the seminar I took, many promises were made about how I would learn more easily if I applied the techniques, and I wanted to test whether these were just empty promises or whether it could actually work.

I then started to learn, practise and apply the memory techniques systematically to various learning situations. In the process, however, I realised that there were a number of practical challenges I came across that were not addressed; I needed something a bit more comprehensive in order to truly test my memory. It left me asking myself:

- How can I best organise my repetition intervals for optimal learning?
- How can I organise the lists of facts I want to learn in a way that would help optimise my memorisation?
- How can I generate random numbers for practising the memorisation of number symbols in the most effective way possible?
- How can I generate a list of random names to practise learning them?
- What are some creative ways I could always carry my learning lists with me in case I have some spare time and want to revise something?

As I encountered each of these challenges, I started creating tools for them using Microsoft Excel. I had previously learnt how to programme macros in Excel so I could automate all the above tasks and tailor the tools to my specific learning needs. Over the years, I have continuously optimised and enlarged them. In order to help you on your learning journey, I want to make these tools available to you. You can download them for free from my website. Whenever we come to a point where I have either built a tool or have some additional content for practice, I will provide the precise download link.

One topic that has always fascinated me has been learning long numbers. A common challenge is to remember as many digits of the number pi (3.141592...) as possible. I have memorised up to 1,600 digits! It is already impressive enough to just know, for example, five hundred digits by heart! I am not saying this to brag here, but only to show you what is possible with the right approach and a bit of practice. Once you have worked through this book, you will find that you, too, can do this.

The more I told others about what was possible for them with the right approach, the more I became aware of the need for these techniques. Schools do not typically teach their students how to learn easily, quickly, and for the long run. This is no reflection on the teachers but a failure of the entire system! I have therefore made it my mission to help fill this gap. I want to make it easier for as many people as possible to get through school, university, professional training, and their professional lives. So, if you like this book and above all find it useful, tell others about it, show them some of the techniques, and invite them to look at the free tips and tools at www.masteroflearning.com. Become part of an ever-growing community of people who use their brains intelligently, achieving so much more by saving time.

What you can expect from this book

When someone does not read beyond the first chapter of a book, I suspect that it is solely because the value of reading the book from beginning to end has not been made readily apparent. So, let me tell you right away how you can personally benefit from reading and working through this book.

In the past, and even today, you probably feel that if you want to learn something, you simply have to repeat things until your memory has understood to some extent that this material is now important. You might do this again the next day and repeat anything you have forgotten. With this rote learning approach, a large part of the material is often gone immediately after the exam for which you have studied. Learning in this way is usually cumbersome, frustrating and only successful in the short term. This often leads to an aversion to learning, knowledge and success at school or university. Worst of all, it leads to the deep-seated belief that you have a poor memory.

Later in your professional life, these rather negative experiences with learning are the reason you don't start learning new things at all, assuming it is too difficult without even having tried. Believe me, I know this only all too well from my own past!

Now, in contrast, imagine what it would be like to be able to remember anything much faster, easier and for longer. When you need to acquire new knowledge at work, you would know precisely how to organise the content and how to learn it quickly and efficiently. Or imagine meeting somebody new. After he has said his name you can memorise it instantly and do not have to ask for it again. And even if you see him again later, you will not only remember his name but also any important details you talked about the previous time.

Let's say you have to give a presentation. Right now, you might be used to the standard approach of having slides with all the facts written out and then just basically reading the content aloud to the class. You may not have considered that it is absolutely possible in this scenario to get by with very few keywords on the slides and recite all the detailed content from memory without hesitation.

With these techniques, it is even possible to learn an entirely new foreign language. You may have hesitated to do this in the past because you may think of it as a daunting task to have to learn so many words. With the memory techniques I will describe in this book, however, you can memorise even the most difficult words and their meanings faster and easier than before. You'll see how these tactics can make learning fifty or more words in an hour a piece of cake.

Positive side effects

These advantages are only the most obvious ones. The faster and easier you are able to learn, the more confident you will become. Got an exam coming up soon? No problem—you know how to prepare yourself! Do you have to do a presentation in front of important customers or senior management? Great—you have all your content safely stored in your memory! You can now rely on memory structures that enable you to recall what you have learned with ease, especially in situations where you may be prone to forgetting one thing or other due to stress or anxiety.

You can expect a higher level of self-confidence from knowing that what you have learnt is safely embedded in your memory and that recalling it will be much easier even under stress. In addition, I have also noted that by applying these learning techniques I have increased my creativity and have started to think in a much more connected way. One reason is that all the techniques presented in this book are based on creating links between pictures. When you regularly look for or have to create connections between sometimes com-pletely unrelated things, you will almost automatically become much more creative over time. For example, consider how you could create a connection between a cloverleaf and a light bulb in your mind. There is no logical connec-tion, so we have to invent something for it. I would connect it by imagining that I am looking for four-leaf clovers in a meadow in the dark and have to turn on a light bulb to see, or perhaps that the thin filament on the inside of a light bulb is the shape of a four-leaf clover. Can you see any other connections between a cloverleaf and light bulb in your mind's eye?

How to use this book

If you actually want to be able to use these memory techniques in your daily life, consider this to be more of a workbook as opposed to something you can just read through once and put aside. I would like to take you on a joint learning journey; along this journey, there are rest areas where you can practise and deepen what you have learned by asking yourself the following questions:

- What have I just learned?
- How could I have applied this lesson in the past?
- How can I apply what I have just learned in the future?

Seminars I have attended in the past would often be two days packed with nothing but theory. The group would spend only a very small portion of the time on exercises, if any at all. Some time ago I went to a seminar that completely reversed this time distribution. Only a third of the time was dedicated to theory, while we spent the rest on practical exercises. I have never learnt so easily in a seminar as I did in this one! This is why I've structured this book the same way in order to support your maximum learning success!

Each chapter is structured as follows:

1. Explanation of the method: the theory
2. Examples: to illustrate the method in practice
3. Exercises: here, it is your turn to try out the method yourself
4. Summary and implementation questions: to help you ensure that you have understood the essential points
5. Tools: in some chapters, I suggest implementation and practice aids with which you can internalize the methods even more easily

I would like to recommend that you read each chapter at least three times: the first time to get to know the content, do the exercises, and answer as many implementation questions as possible; the second time to check the answers to the implementation questions and answer questions you could not answer the first time round; and the third time to deepen what you have learned.

My own experience with these kind of implementation questions so far has been that if I read the content once and then have to answer the questions, I cannot necessarily answer all of them. I then read through it a second time and notice things that I might have previously overlooked or considered unimportant. If I have specific questions in mind, I read the text with a different mindset and recognise things I did not notice the first time. Reading the text a third time helps solidify new insights and enables me to apply what I have just read more and more as I go.

Basically, you cannot learn the memory techniques from mere reading! As I will introduce to you in the next chapter, most of the techniques presented here are based on prepared models that you learn first and then use as a basis for learning new content. You need to know these prepared models well, and this requires some practice. But don't worry, I can help you with this. As previously mentioned, at various points throughout the book I will provide you with links to free tools that you can use to practise the techniques. I have found practicing the techniques for five to ten minutes every day for two weeks is enough to feel comfortable enough to start using them.

As you apply these techniques to the exercises, you can assess how well each of them works for you. The more systematically you do this, the stronger your confidence in these techniques—and ultimately your own ability to learn—will become. This increased self-confidence provides you with more motivation to not only work through the book to the end but also to approach further learning projects with self-confidence, thus increasing your learning success.

When I went through the contents of this book with others, it was my experience that it takes about twenty hours of pure practice to internalize the techniques from this book and be able to apply them well. Depending on what kind of learning projects you have in front of you, you will recover this time investment quickly. In my experience, the absolute minimum you can expect from this course is to double your learning speed!

But beware of perfectionism. Perfectionism arouses aggression, and aggression reduces your fun in learning; the stress associated with stressful learning then reduces your success! We will come back to this in a later chapter, but mistakes are perfectly normal—often even helpful—so perfectionism has no place in learning. This is especially true if the pursuit of perfection means you are waiting for the perfect time to start learning instead of just going for it!

Wait no longer; start with an entrance test that will help you determine how good your memory already is and where there is still room for improvement.

Entrance test

This test is not about getting everything right; in fact, it is quite unlikely that you will. Rather, it should allow you to take stock of your current situation objectively so that at the end of the book you can see how much you have improved through your newly learned memory techniques.

You will be given the opportunity to repeat the test at the end of the course and compare your results. You will see that with the help of these techniques, you will be able to remember much more in the same time—often even the complete contents of the test. This level of skill can be your new normal state of learning! So, let's get started.

How does the test work?

Take a pen, some paper and a timer, for example on your mobile phone. Sit down in a quiet place where you will not be disturbed.

Read the instructions carefully before each exercise. As soon as you have finished, set the timer to the specified time. Once it starts, memorise as much of the information as possible. When the timer has finished, count backwards in increments of 7 starting at 100, i.e. 100, 93, 86, and so on. When you get to 2, write down all the things you recall from the exercise and then check how many of them you got right.

When you have done all the exercises, add up your points for your overall score. Write down your results in the table at the end of the test. You may write them on a separate sheet of paper instead if you prefer, being sure to put this paper back in your book. If you have the audiobook or electronic version of the book, just take a screenshot or picture of your results with your phone so you can consult them later. You will need them after working through the book to see how much progress you have made.

I. Shopping list

Duration: 1 minute; maximum score: 20

Remember as many of the things on this shopping list as possible. For each correct item, you get one point, another one for the correct position on the list.

1. asparagus
2. hair gel
3. tomatoes
4. toilet paper
5. dog food
6. frozen pizza
7. coloured pencils
8. cheese
9. bread roll
10. pack of muesli

II. Abstract words

Duration: 3 minutes; maximum score: 40

Learn the following twenty words in the order given. For each correct word, you get one point. For the correct position on the list, you get another point.

1. to walk
2. faithful
3. abstract
4. crutch
5. freedom
6. fast
7. pandemic
8. traffic sign
9. fuel
10. future
11. basement
12. sinner
13. oxygen
14. oil rig
15. platelets
16. gravity
17. reactive
18. sluggish
19. ballistics
20. repetition

III. Telephone numbers

Duration: 3 minutes; maximum score: 30

This part is about learning different phone numbers. For each correct number, you get five points; when you allocate it to the correct person, you get another point.

1. Uncle Jim: 5375643
2. Aunt Anne: 787 3923408
3. Mrs Whithead: 499879
4. Frank: 243258
5. Daddy: 31857

IV. Vocabulary

Duration: 3 minutes; maximum score: 30

Learn the following fantasy words. For each correct translation, you get three points if the spelling is correct. For each letter spelled incorrectly, there is a one-point deduction per word.

book - kompoll
car - rilkamber
freedom - sockduber
rain - bneggens
trampoline - yambup
lawn - zellmon
pen - keskrimber
telephone - pulgaber
barbecue - prinvia
ball - bassnute

V. Faces and names

Duration: 2 minutes; maximum score: 40

Learn the first and last names of the following people and their faces. For each correctly remembered first name and surname, you get two points each; for each name you match to the correct face, you get one point. For each misspelled letter, there is a one-point deduction per name.

Theo Clark   Mariah Cooper Gabriel Turner Anthony Scott

Elaina Ward   Dylan Hill   Angelina King   Sage Watson

VI. Task list

Duration: 2 minutes; maximum score: 20

Memorise the following ten tasks. Again, there is one point given for each correctly remembered task and another for the correct position on the list.

1. Buy a gift for Paula
2. Pick up shirts from the dry cleaner's
3. Take letters to the post office
4. Practise piano
5. Clean up the garage
6. Mow the lawn
7. Check children's homework
8. Go shopping
9. Order a printer cartridge
10. Repair bike

VII. Facts about Arnold Schwarzenegger

Duration: 1.5 minutes; maximum score: 20

Here are some interesting facts about Arnold Schwarzenegger. For each correctly remembered fact, independent of the order, you get two points.

1. Born in 1947
2. Birthplace Thal, Austria
3. Has BA in International Economics
4. Since 1983 US citizen
5. 1967 first Mr Universe
6. First Terminator Film 1984
7. Republican
8. 38th Governor of California
9. Eats mostly vegan food
10. Lives in Los Angeles

Review

I. Shopping list

For each correct item you get one point. For each correct position on the list, you get another point.

1. _____

2. _____

3. _____

4. _____

5. _____

6. _____

7. _____

8. _____

9. _____

10. _____

Number of points: _____

II. Abstract words

For each correct translation, you get three points if the spelling is correct. For each letter spelled incorrectly, there is a one-point deduction per word.

1. _____

2. _____

3. _____

4. _____

5. _____

6. _____

7. _____

8. _____

9. _____

10. _____

11. _____

12. _____

13. _____

14. _____

15. _____

16. _____

17. _____

18. _____

19. _____

20. _____

Number of points: _____

III. Telephone numbers

For each correct number, you get five points. When you allocate it to the correct person you get another point.

1. Mrs Whithead: _____

2. Uncle Jim: _____

3. Frank: _____

4. Mummy: _____

5. Aunt Anne: _____

Number of points: _____

IV. Vocabulary

For each correct translation, you get three points if the spelling is correct. For each letter spelled incorrectly, there is a one-point deduction per word.

ball - _____

lawn - _____

_____ - rilkamber

barbecue - _____

_____ - pulgaber

freedom - _____

_____ - bneggens

trampoline - _____

_____ - keskrimber

_____ - kompoll

Number of points: _____

V. Faces and names

For each correctly remembered first name and surname, you get two points. For matching each to the correct person, you will get another point. For each misspelled letter, there is a one-point deduction per name.

Number of points:

VI. Task list

You get one point for each correctly remembered task and another one for the correct position on the list.

1. _____

2. _____

3. _____

4. _____

5. _____

6. _____

7. _____

8. _____

9. _____

10. _____

Number of points: _____

VII. Facts about Arnold Schwarzenegger

For each correctly remembered fact, independent of the order, you get two points.

1. _____

2. _____

3. _____

4. _____

5. _____

6. _____

7. _____

8. _____

9. _____

10. _____

Number of points: _____

Overall result

I.   Shopping list   _____points

II.   Abstract words   _____points

III.   Telephone numbers   _____points

IV.   Vocabulary   _____points

V.   Faces and names   _____points

VI.   Task list   _____points

VII.   Facts about Arnold Schwarzenegger   _____points

TOTAL NUMBER OF POINTS: _____ **out of 200 possible points**

CHAPTER 2

THE BASICS OF LEARNING

How to survive with pictures

Our brain, and therefore our memory, has very much been shaped by the characteristics that have supported human survival over the course of our evolutionary history. Let us take a look back at the early days of mankind, when humans still lived in caves and hunted mammoths. At that time, the top priority was their own survival and the survival of their own genes, i.e. their family. The challenge was, among other things, to find sufficient food. That meant knowing where the mammoths were and where they could be hunted, where the clean water could be found, where the good or poisonous berries were and, of course, where the sabre-toothed tigers or other dangerous predators had attacked the last time. To do this, these places and the paths to them could only be remembered by looking at the landscape and finding visual cues such as large boulders or trees, rivers and other landmarks. There was no such thing as a signpost or Google Maps yet—or any maps for that matter. And also, the way back to the cave had to be remembered, otherwise the survival of the clan would be in danger.

In short, the people who had a very strong visual memory were those more likely to survive—and thus whose genes were therefore more likely to be passed on. Even today, visual learning works best. We can remember images such as a face much better than abstract content, such as numbers or names; therefore, all memory techniques presented in this book are picture-based. This allows you to transform the learning content, no matter how abstract it may be, into concrete pictures that you can envisage in your mind. Only in this way is your brain able to remember all kinds of content—even in large quantities—quickly, easily and permanently. Picture-based learning is therefore brain-friendly learning.

One of the easiest applications of the picture-based learning method is telling stories; it is also the one we are generally most familiar with, so let us look at it in the next section.

Learning with stories

In the world of literature, there are many works that try to teach readers and listeners something through their stories. The most famous examples are probably the parables in the Bible. Jesus frequently used them to teach his followers. Similarly, many fairy tales and fables were passed on from one generation to the next to teach the younger generation the principles and cultural values of sticking together and living well. Stories have been used throughout all cultures and times. As Grant Graves puts it: "The path to learning wanders through a good story."

We, too, can use storytelling to remember things we want to learn because a story connects a series of pictures with some logical link. Let me demonstrate what I mean with the following example.

While you read the following story, please try to imagine it in all its details and as vividly as possible. To do so, it is best to read it out loud.

> *You hold a hammer in your right hand, a heavy piece of wood in the other hand and because you have twenty nails in your mouth, you cannot speak. Since you need to ask your friend about lunch, you place everything on the ground. To keep the nails from magically disappearing, you stick them neatly in a row on a stripe of duct tape and attach the stripe to a plastic bucket that contains white paint. After lunch you take a broom that has one end that looks like a screwdriver and you use this to open a light bulb and put some batteries in it.*

Read through the story once more and try to remember every detail of it.

What do you hold in the one hand; what in the other?
Why can you not talk to your friend directly?
What is in the bucket?
What do you use to open the light bulb?
What do you put into it?
Then, recite the story and see how well you can remember the details.

This story is about a list of items you want to purchase at the hardware store. By linking the items together in a story, you have a brain-friendly way of remembering all the items. When you are actually in the store, you just need to go through the story again, see which items come up in the story and then select them one by one.

Here is the story again with the relevant items highlighted:

> *You hold a **hammer** in your right hand, a heavy piece of **wood** in the other hand and because you have twenty **nails** in your mouth, you cannot speak. Since you need to ask your friend about lunch, you place everything on the ground. To keep the nails from magically disappearing, you stick them neatly in a row on a stripe of **duct tape** and attach the stripe to a **plastic bucket** that contains **white paint**. After lunch you take a **broom** that has one end that looks like a **screwdriver** and you use this to open a **light bulb** and put some **batteries** in it.*

So, your shopping list for the hardware store looks like this:

- hammer
- wood
- nails
- duct tape
- plastic bucket
- white paint
- broom
- screwdriver

- light bulb
- batteries

Now it is your turn to test how well the story worked for you. On the empty lines below, write down the shopping list as well as you can remember it. When you have finished, count how many items you could remember.

1. _____

2. _____

3. _____

4. _____

5. _____

6. _____

7. _____

8. _____

9. _____

10. _____

How well did you remember them? Did you get them all? If not, do not worry; just go back to the story and revisit the part where the images were not clear enough. You could add some more detail, emotion or dynamic to that particular part but try to keep it as simple as possible, only adding where it is needed. Then try it once more. With the help of the story you will be able to remember the shopping list quite easily.

Let's try another story. Here it is:

> *A water bottle is attached to a balloon and rises into the sky.*
> *All of a sudden, a whole swarm of small batteries come flying*
> *at it and pierce the balloon so that the water bottle falls down*

onto a bear who looks completely bored. He jumps up, gets into a car and drives along the road next to a river. Suddenly he sees a knight in a rowing boat together with a big, brown ox and they are both brushing their teeth under a flashy green and red neon sign.

Now read the story again and replay it in your imagination. Again, pay attention to every detail.

What happens to the balloon in the sky?
How does the bear look?
Where does he drive?
What does he see there?
What do the knight and the ox do?
What is above their heads?
As soon as you can retell the story, please read on.

Congratulations! The story is about the first ten chemical elements as they occur in the periodic table. By remembering this story, you will be able to list the first ten elements. Here is the story again with the highlighted keywords:

*A **water** bottle is attached to a **balloon** and rises into the sky. All of a sudden, a whole swarm of small **batteries** come flying at it and pierce the balloon so that the water bottle falls down onto a **bear** who looks completely **bored**. He jumps up, gets into a **car** and drives along the road next to a river. Suddenly he sees a **knight** in a **rowing** boat together with a big, brown **ox** and they are both **brushing** their **teeth** under a flashy green and red **neon** sign.*

The symbols used in the story translate to the elements in the following way:

1. water - Hydrogen
2. balloon - Helium, a balloon is often filled with Helium to make it rise
3. batteries - Lithium: batteries often use Lithium
4. bear - Beryllium: starts with same sound
5. bored - Boron
6. car - Carbon
7. knight and row - Nitrogen
8. ox - Oxygen
9. brushing teeth - Fluorine: a key ingredient in many toothpastes
10. neon - Neon

Depending on how well you already know the chemical elements, some will have been easier to remember and others more difficult, but if you go through the list a few times, you will notice that the pictures become more and more familiar. You can also remember the slightly lesser known elements like Beryllium well.

Now write down the ten chemical elements in the right order:

1. _____

2. _____

3. _____

4. _____

5. _____

6. _____

7. _____

8. _____

9. _____

10. _____

The advantage of using stories to link different items in the correct order is that it is quite simple and above all easy to learn and use. Most of us have had stories told to us since childhood, and so we are quite familiar with hearing and even creating our own stories. Before we look at another even more powerful method for learning lists, it is important for you to understand some very fundamental ways in which our brains handle information. In the next section I will show you why thinking and learning in pictures is the most brain-friendly way to learn, store and recall information so that your learning process is faster and easier.

The principles of picture-based learning

Telling stories to remember a list of items is a simple and very useful approach that works very well, as participants in my workshops keep telling me. In order to use this and the other picture-based approaches, we need to dive deeper into how the techniques work and how you can become proficient in them.

So, what are the general principles you need to understand and practise in the beginning? First of all, you always have to transform what you want to learn into pictures. Sometimes this is very easy, like when we want to remember a list of items such as a shopping list. Here, the learning contents are already available as clear pictures. Anyone can imagine an apple, a bicycle or a frozen pizza. With more abstract contents or unknown words, it becomes a bit more difficult. Or can you imagine "sophistication" or "contentment" as simple pictures? If you can't, do not worry. This book will show you exactly how this is done as we dive deeper into the methods.

Once you have a mental picture of your learning material, you need a system for storing the learning content so that it can easily be retrieved later. I like to compare this to the cloakroom in a theatre: if I have a jacket with me, I go to the cloakroom where a nice man or lady takes my jacket, hangs it onto a hook, and gives me a cloakroom ticket with a number on it. If I want my jacket back after the performance, I just go to the cloakroom, hand in the ticket with the number and get my jacket back without difficulty.

Imagine if there were no such well-structured coat racks with the numbers on them! Then maybe the visitors of the theatre would throw their jackets onto a big pile and the one who wants their jacket back first after the performance will have real difficulties finding it! This is a good picture of what happens when you try to remember something through rote learning. You repeat the same information over and over again until it only kind of sticks in your brain, and only for a short while.

The techniques I will show you in this book are therefore structured in much the same way as the coat rack in the theatre: there is a prepared structure in which the learning content is stored, so that it is easily and quickly available after the performance, so to speak, when you want to be able to retrieve it again. There are also the cloakroom tickets, which essentially make the connection between the learning content and the hook where the content is stored, like our jacket. As a third, additional element, we need a hanger loop on the jacket so that the jacket can be hung on the hook and that is the visualisation of the learning content.

Each hook of these coat racks is, again, a picture, so that you now have two pictures—one for the new content, and one for the hook. Now you still need a bridge that connects the two pictures. For example, if the picture for the hook is a car and you want to remember an apple from a shopping list, then you now look for a connection between an apple and a car, e.g. you run over the apple with your car and then imagine in your mind's eye how the apple juice flows over the road and some pieces of apple stick to the tyre of the car. This may seem a bit strange at first, but this strangeness is precisely what makes it memorable and helps the brain to recognize that this combination of apple and car is worth remembering.

I call this approach the PC method, or the picture-connection method. When you use pictures to learn something, you have a clear visual idea of what you want to learn and thus can remember it much more easily! This approach might seem a bit unusual at first, but it truly works!

The easiest application for this is when you want to learn something easy—something that is possible to remember using a single picture, like the apple in the example above. A picture of an apple is sufficient; it's easy. But more often than not, the things we want to learn can be a bit more complex. Let's say you not only need to remember that you should buy apples but also that they should be red (not green!) and that there should be five apples (not eight, not two!). Not only do you need to picture the apple being run over by a car, but also something to help you remember "red" and "5". A mental picture for red could be blood and a picture for five could be a hand (because a hand has five fingers).

Now, imagine yourself running over the apple with the car, but instead of apple juice, blood flows out of the apple and then you pick up the remains of the apple with your hand and see exactly where the blood came from. Now when you are at the supermarket and go through your shopping list in your mind, you will not only remember that you should buy apples but also that they should be red (because of the blood) and that it should not be eight or two, but five (because of the fingers on your hand).

As you can see, the solution is simply to connect the additional pictures that are needed to remember the colour and quantity, and then make a little story out of them. A story is, in essence, nothing but a sequence of pictures connected one after the other.

Since this is such an important basic element of picture-based memory techniques, here are some exercises that you can do to practise the PC method.

Exercise

Connect the following word pairs by creating a little story like the example above with the apple and the car.

glass - stone
guitar - lamp
grass - rocket
book - cloud
laptop - cushion
steering wheel - pen
knife - tree
diamond - digger
lens - wave
bucket - rifle

Now go through the list below and add the second word.

glass - _____

guitar - _____

_____ - rocket

book - _____

laptop - _____

_____ - pen

_____ - tree

_____ - digger

lens - _____

_____ - rifle

Aside from the PC method, there is another important method in learning called the UK method. It is based on the concept that combining something unknown ("U") with something known ("K") optimises the learning experience. The "known" is a prepared structure—much like the coat rack.

Unknown - Connection - Known

You can prepare these structures. Once you have memorised them, they are your known structures to which you can attach the new content you want to learn: the unknown, as described above in the picture of the theatre cloak-room. Usually this is possible without much effort. Throughout this book, I will introduce you to a number of concrete structures and most importantly, explain how you can create such prepared structures yourself. Once you have become familiar with these structures, you will be able to use them successfully in many situations.

The Body List

Let us apply these two principles now to a very concrete situation and see how it works in practise. Assume you want to learn a shopping list by heart as a first example. The first step is that you need to have a prepared list to which you can connect the various items on your shopping list. Something that you always have with you is your body, therefore it is particularly suitable as a memory system and you will use it to create your first known structure.

The principle is very simple: You take a part of your body and connect it mentally with the numbers from 1 to 10 as follows:

1 - feet
2 - knees
3 - thigh
4 - behind
5 - belly
6 - chest
7 - mouth
8 - nose
9 - eyes
10 - hair

The easiest way to learn this is to stand up and say the numbers out loud while touching the corresponding body part. Once you have done this a few times, you should remember which part of the body is which number easily. It is best to repeat this a few times over the next few days since you will be using this body list quite a bit in the future.

Now you have a picture for each of the numbers from one to ten and you can use them to learn a shopping list as a first exercise.

Shopping with the Body List

Let us assume you want to be able to remember the following shopping list:

1. pumpkin
2. paper
3. water bottle
4. tomatoes
5. peas
6. butter
7. onions
8. bread
9. milk
10. eggs

In order to connect the body parts (and thus the numbers from 1 to 10) in such a way that you can easily remember the list, you now have to tell yourself little stories about how the things on the shopping list are related to your body parts, i.e. you will apply the PC principle. This could look something like this:

1. you kick your foot against a pumpkin and as a consequence your foot hurts
2. you kneel on sheets of paper so your knees don't get dirty
3. you balance a water bottle on your thigh
4. you put a tomato between your buttocks (don't press too hard!)
5. you have a pea in your belly button
6. you spread butter all over your chest
7. you bite into a raw onion and it tastes very strong
8. a freshly baked bread floats in front of your nose and you breathe in the fresh smell with pleasure
9. you have to cry, but instead of tears milk comes out of your eyes
10. an egg bursts on your head and runs slowly down your hair

Now it is your turn to see how well you have memorised the above pictures. Can you recall all 10 items from the shopping list?

1 - (feet): _____

2 - (knees): _____

3 - (thigh): _____

4 - (behind): _____

5 - (belly): _____

6 - (chest): _____

7 - (mouth): _____

8 - (nose): _____

9 - (eyes): _____

10 - (hair): _____

If there are connection pictures here that do not work well for you, just create your own. Either way, it is always best to create your own pictures. This can take you more time to do it, especially in the beginning. Until you feel fully comfortable with this method, it might be easier to practise with somebody else's pictures.

Once you have memorised the individual pictures with sufficient intensity, you should be able to recite most, if not all, of the ten items in the correct order. With a shopping list, the order is of course (at least usually) irrelevant, but with the Body List you have learned the correct order automatically.

Now test yourself and see how many of the things you can recite from memory. If you can remember at least eight things, it is already working well. If you did less than eight the first time, that's not too bad; just revise the pictures you couldn't remember the first time around. Below I will show you some reinforcement techniques that can help you strengthen the pictures and thus remember them more easily. Afterwards, test yourself again and you will see that it already works much better.

As with so many things in life, repetition is the master of skill. Once you have understood this basic principle and have practised a few times with different examples, then every future application will become easier and easier! The only mistake you can make is to become too impatient and give up. I have never had a student who did *not* improve their memory using the Body List, so why should *you* of all people be the first?

If you now try to learn a second shopping list with the help of the Body List, you will probably start to mix up the pictures and not be able to tell the two lists apart. That is perfectly understandable! You do not only have one connection to the foot, but now you have two! And since you cannot distinguish the one from the other, you run the concrete risk of confusing the lists. So, if you want to learn more than ten things, you need a longer body list. This is what we will focus on in the next chapter.

Before we do so, however, I would like to share some ways to make your pictures and stories become even more memorable and therefore stick more easily in your memory.

Bodybuilding for your pictures

Before we start with the first exercises, I would like to give you some useful hints on how you can significantly increase the power and strength of your memory pictures, stories and connections.

Learning with all the senses

Each picture or story is easier to remember if you use as many of your senses as possible. In the example of the apple above, you can easily picture an apple because you can see it by using your eyesight. But what about the other senses: hearing, feeling, smelling and tasting? What does it sound like when the car drives over the apple? After you pick up the apple remains, how do the apple pieces feel in your hand? What does the apple smell like? And if you tasted the blood, would it taste a bit like iron, like normal blood, or does it just look like blood but taste like apple juice?

If you use these sensations in your pictures and stories, it becomes even more real for your brain and it wants to create a memory. By using different senses different parts of the brain are used and this helps the brain to store information more easily.

This effect will be even stronger if you make the pictures in colour instead of black and white and if you add more dynamics, i.e. movement. It might be less memorable to imagine a dark grey car standing motionless somewhere than if you imagine it's bright yellow and driving along a motorway at full speed.

Show feelings!

Have you ever watched a film that really inspired you and was only about numbers, facts and figures? Probably not! All good films take us on a journey through changing emotional states. Every good film has drama, tension, tragedy, horror, and pain at the climax. These themes usually resolve themselves by the end of the film into harmony, love, joy, happiness and a certain amount of relief. Why should your learning stories be any different?

If you create pictures and stories for yourself to remember new content, use the power of emotions to make them even more memorable for you. Don't just imagine stepping on tomatoes with your foot, although this mental picture might be enough to connect *foot* and *tomato*. Let a short film play before your inner eye that shows the following scene: how you step into the tomatoes and the tomatoes bursting. Imagine how disgusting it would feel as the juice from the tomato spreads between your toes. Let's say that you need to remember something involving a rope, so you might want to imagine tying a rope around your stomach. As you do this, feel how the rope becomes tighter and tighter around you, maybe rubbing a little and slowly starting to hurt. In another instance, you might like to connect *flower* and *lamp*. How about picturing yourself putting your partner's favourite flowers into a vase and placing them in a dark corner of the living room? Only when she enters the room do you turn on the lamp, which illuminates the flowers. Your partner is totally surprised. A smile appears on her face and she looks at you with love. How is that for a strong connection?

I could give you many more examples, but I think the principle has become clear. The more emotional the story, the more memorable it is. Use the whole range of human emotion, including negative emotions like hate, violence and pain—or even those that are generally not spoken about in public like eroticism and sexuality. The most important thing is that the pictures are memorable for you personally.

Make it personal

When you are learning it is very helpful to put yourself in the centre of the action. If the car is driving on the motorway as in the example above, imagine that you are driving it yourself. You feel the steering wheel in your hands, you look through the windshield, you are paying attention to the traffic, you feel the pressure on your foot when you step on the gas pedal and you feel the acceleration all over your body. If you make yourself the centre of your stories, it is usually easier to access your full range of feelings.

Learning is a deeply personal matter. If you use your personal associations by creating pictures and stories that remind you of experiences from your personal past, then you will remember even more of what you have learned. After all, you have always experienced your past emotionally. Pictures and stories based on your own experiences are usually more emotional and therefore easier to learn than those that you have just artificially made up.

Let's assume you want to combine *apple pie* and *pliers*. You could just simply imagine yourself lifting a piece of apple pie with pliers; however, the image will become much stronger for you if you remember, for example, how your child smiled at you the other day, perhaps in a situation where you gave her a great gift or did her a favour. If you now apply that to the image of serving her a piece of apple pie on her plate with pliers, *and* it's exactly the same apple pie that you or your partner always bake, then you have put yourself in the centre of the story. Using memories and incorporating emotions from your own experiences will help you remember these mental pictures significantly!

The emotional closeness we have with our children, partners, parents, siblings and friends can be used in our stories to establish a more personal connection and make a picture even more memorable than if the image were generated randomly without any emotional connection to it.

The devil is in the details

Another helpful technique is to create an even more detailed picture or story—especially if it's a picture that may be trickier to recall during your first few repetitions. Sometimes the connection does not fit well enough, which creates difficulties in linking the two symbols (the "known" and the "unknown") into a picture or short story. The more detail is added, the more concrete the picture becomes. It is therefore easier for you to learn as the additional detail makes the connection clearer and stronger.

Sometimes, when you are looking for a picture to represent a fact you want to commit to memory, a personal picture may automatically appear in your mind's eye. You might have a direct personal reference to it and can use it easily. If this is not the case, it is always a good idea to start with simple pictures. When you go through your repetitions, you will notice which pictures are already sufficiently embedded in your memory and which ones are not. Wherever the current picture is not enough, simply add more details to it. Make your little story slightly longer and more dramatic. It is best to do this by intensifying your emotions and using more of your senses.

When I talked about the example of the apple and the car, I used this particular approach and showed you that it works quite nicely. Even if the details that you add to your picture or story are not very emotional, the details will always add more strength to the connection. And in a certain way, there is no detail without using your senses. If the car is red, you see it. If it is loud, you hear it. If it leaves behind some nasty fumes, you smell it. (You get the idea.)

Avoid confusion

Another difficulty that you might occasionally encounter is that for some pictures there are several possibilities when you translate them back to their original meaning. This can happen, for instance, when there are synonyms, i.e. different words for the same concept. The other day I wanted to remember the term "wealthy" and was able to associate the word with Warren Buffett, who is probably the most famous investor of our times. I have read enough stories and seen his picture often enough that I have a clear image in my mind of what he looks like. Unfortunately, when I went through my first repetition to see how well I had remembered it, I didn't think of the term "wealthy" but of "rich", which is almost the same thing, but the exact word was important, so I needed another detail to remember "wealthy" instead of "rich". In this case, it was a whale. I pictured Warren Buffett riding on an enormous whale, throwing about his money. The whale reminded me I was looking for a word starting with "w" and then I had no problem recalling "wealthy" instead of "rich".

Make it strange funny nonsense

Many of the examples I have used so far will never exist as actual situations in real life. You might be thinking: *An elderly billionaire riding on a whale? An apple with blood pouring out of it? Please! These are completely nonsensical images!* But this is the secret to learning right here. Everything that is completely nonsensical, absurd and far-fetched is simply memorable. The Germans have an even easier way to remember this since their word "merkwürdig" means both "strange" and "memorable". "Merken" in German means "to remember" and "würdig" means "worthy" or "worthwhile", so "merk-würdig" literally means that something is worth remembering. So, this German word describes very well why the nonsensical helps us to learn: it is so far outside the norm that it is not only strange but also remarkable, thus worthy of remembering! Our brain receives millions of impressions every day and has to decide what to keep, and what to get rid of. Anything that is so far from the ordinary will attract more attention and curiosity and will therefore be kept, while all the other unremarkable impressions and pictures will not stay in your mind for very long (at least not at a conscious level).

Creating these extraordinary pictures and stories also has a nice side effect as mentioned before. Besides the pure memory effect, it also challenges and encourages your creativity and your networked thinking to create such nonsensical stories, and so you will find that you will become more creative in other areas after you have practised and applied these techniques for a while. Children find this approach to learning particularly easy, since they are most often still caught up in their own world of stories and tales that they invent or relive when they are playing. In this way, it is often easier for them to come up with creative connections between two or more pictures. So, let's be more like children again, have fun while learning and enter the playful world of learning stories with joy!

It is logical!

Having written above about emotions, egoism and nonsense, which, if used correctly, can enhance the learning effect, I don't want to forget about good old logic here. If something is easily comprehensible and conclusive, our brain understands the connections which in turn means that it inserts the new content into something familiar. This brings us back to the UK method of connecting the new, unknown item to something known for better recall. So, wherever I can manage to connect the new content logically with known facts or structures, I have opportunities for strong memory hooks.

A simple example of this would be telephone numbers that differ only slightly. In companies, for example, there is a general number that usually ends with -0 at the end. If I know the extension of the person I want to talk to, which is usually only 3 or 4 digits long, I can remember a whole series of longer telephone numbers by learning the company number and then the short extensions for each person. Some companies have a similar pattern with their mobile phone numbers.

How would you go about memorising the following 22-digit number?

$$1123581321345589144233$$

At first sight it does not seem very easy, even if there are numbers that repeat themselves from time to time (also this is in itself already a kind of mini-structure). It suddenly becomes easy when you notice that each number is actually just the sum of the two numbers that come before it. We start with 1, and since there is no number in front of it, we take $0 + 1$, which is 1 for the second number. Then $1 + 1 = 2$, then $1 + 2 = 3$, $2 + 3 = 5$ and so on. Knowing this, it then becomes very easy to remember the long number, even if the number keeps going, since you can keep on adding up each two preceding numbers.

Thus, recognizing and learning structures wherever we find them is an important simplification of the necessary learning process and should definitely be used. It can also be combined with other techniques. We will come to this later when we go into learning long numbers by heart.

By the way, with regard to the use of logic, pseudo-logic also works very well. In some cases, I can pretend that there is a logical connection, even if in reality it does not exist. For example, Charlemagne was born in 747 AD. When you think of the number 747, which picture comes directly to your mind? Right, a Boeing 747, which is a pretty big plane. Of course, there is no logical connection between the year Charlemagne was born and the name of this plane, but since the numbers are the same and the plane is so well known, I can use the PC method to create a little story that is very easy to remember. I imagine Charlemagne getting off the plane and waving benevolently to the waiting crowd. If I want to add a little more detail, I can also imagine that he has a heavy crown on his head, there is a light breeze, and the crowd cheers him on. But basically, the picture of the king stepping out of the plane is enough to remind me of his year of birth.

Should I find out that I have incorrectly recalled 747 as his coronation year (correct year would be 800 AD) or his year of death (814 AD), then I could add as a detail that he is holding a little baby in his arms as he stands there in the doorway.

Practising picture-based learning

The better you become at visualising the images, symbols and stories you need to apply the PC method, the more easily they can be anchored in your memory. Many of us have created our own stories while playing as children, but I know it is not always so easy for us to do as adults. While some participants in my seminars are able to get started in creating their pictures and stories and can immediately apply the techniques successfully, other participants are not yet ready. The good news for all those who feel the same way is that if it doesn't work from the beginning, you can still make progress very quickly with just a little practice!

Let's do an exercise so you can see what I mean. Imagine you are driving a car and you are sitting behind the wheel. Next to you, in the passenger seat, is a lion. How unexpected! What exactly does the lion look like? How big is the lion? What colour is it? Is it a real lion or a cartoon? Where are its legs? What is it doing with its tail? Does the lion fit comfortably in the car, or is it so big that you both are squeezed in so tightly and you hardly have any room to move? Does it talk? Does it otherwise make noise? What does it smell like? Does it try to eat you?

How has your image of the lion changed while you were asking yourself all these questions? Has it become clearer? Did you have your eyes open or closed when you imagined the lion? Try it the other way. Does it work better now?

Let's try another exercise. Imagine standing on a narrow board high above a deep ravine. You look down. What do you see there? Do you feel how the board swings slightly? Do you feel the wind? How deep is the ravine below you? What do you see on the ground? Are there plants? What about animals? Do people walk there? Is there a road?

The more you try to go into this picture with all your senses and looking at the details, the clearer the picture should become. The more you focus on the picture through the detailed questions, the more precisely you should perceive everything. Even if you don't see clear pictures the first time, you can practise the ability to see such pictures with your inner eye through similar exercises. If you are not yet satisfied, simply use a few quiet moments to create your own pictures and scenarios, no matter where you are right now.

If you have no imagination at all, you can also do the following exercise: take a picture of a person, place or thing and look at the picture once. Ask yourself a question similar to the ones I asked you above. After two to three minutes, put the picture aside and close your eyes. How well can you see the picture now? Try to remember the details. Then, open your eyes again and see how close you were. Repeat the exercise with another picture.

Whether you are able to picture things in your mind or not, it will require some practice to get familiar with the techniques introduced in this book. Any learning process will have parts that are relatively easy and others that are more challenging and require more practice. One thing that is completely unavoidable, however, is making mistakes. Anyone who learns anything new will make mistakes in the beginning. When you learn something new and then repeat it for the first time, there will invariably be things that you simply cannot remember. This is not only normal, but there simply is no way around it!

The way you deal with these mistakes can have quite an impact on your learning progress, so let us look at how best to do so.

How to deal with mistakes

When young children learn new things at the very beginning of their lives, such as walking, they do so by observing others and then trying to imitate them. We adults walk on two legs, so the toddler wants to do that, too. He starts to pull himself up wherever he can, and, in the beginning, he always falls down again. Even if it hurts sometimes, he continues, because the surrounding adults comfort him whenever he is crying and applaud him when he makes even the least bit of progress. In this way, the child learns to just keep trying until it works. There are no minimum requirements, test plans or target agreements here yet; the child is simply allowed to try it out.

In school, the focus shifts more towards avoiding mistakes and thus gives mistakes the negative meaning that they have today for many of us. For example, when I took spelling tests in primary school, the grades were distributed according to the number of mistakes: the fewer mistakes I made, the better the grade I got. So, it was not about the number of correct words, but about avoiding the wrong words. And this was the case until the end of school; for example, in foreign language classes where part of the evaluation was always the error rate, the teacher divided the number of my mistakes by the number of words and the fewer mistakes I made, the better my grade was. At the time, this gave us (the students) the impression that learning at school is all about avoiding mistakes, and it is no different today.

But you have to make an important distinction: while tests and exams are about avoiding mistakes and getting it right, mistakes do play an important role, if not an essential one, in learning and are completely unavoidable!

If you have memorised something initially and make mistakes when you quiz yourself for the first few times, then this is not a big deal at all but simply an indication that you have to revise these points more intensively. I have given you some hints earlier on how you can design your learning pictures in a way that helps you remember them more easily. Now you have concrete ideas and recommendations on how to proceed in this situation. You are not at the mercy of your mistakes anymore!

The meaning you give to a mistake also has a great influence on how you deal with it. If the same mistake happens over and over again and you haven't changed much about your picture, know that you still have more arrows in your quiver and that you can easily change it.

It became especially clear to me what influence the negative evaluation of a mistake has on your learning success when I started coaching the adolescent son of friends of mine. He was trying to learn a story for remembering the countries of America but made a small mistake relatively at the beginning. Unfortunately, he did not see it as a small mistake that he could correct easily; instead he got completely annoyed and could not focus on the story anymore. When I explained to him that mistakes in learning are perfectly okay and even unavoidable, he relaxed after a while, went through the story again with me and was able to retell it afterwards without any mistakes.

Often it is even the case that when you make initial mistakes, you will remember it all the better later on. This is similar to a broken bone. When the bone has healed, the connection is stronger at this point than it was before breaking and therefore will not break again in the same spot. It surprises me again and again when I realise that this is similar to learning with mistakes. Now that I know this, I am even happy when something like this happens to me, because I then simply check my learning picture, change it slightly if necessary and then expect that I can reproduce it safely next time. Rarely am I disappointed!

Here are a few concrete hints regarding your handling of mistakes while learning:

Be aware that mistakes in the beginning cannot be avoided at all

When you are learning something and everything is new, you need some repetitions until the brain recognizes that the material is important enough to remember. Once you have learnt something new and start quizzing yourself to see if you can remember it, you will not yet be able to remember everything and thus you make "mistakes". So, you should explicitly allow yourself to make these mistakes in the beginning (and also in later repetitions)! My own rule is that I allow myself to make five mistakes before I even have the feeling that the material is a bit more difficult at the moment and I have to learn it differently. In this way, I am relaxed while I am learning and can learn faster. It doesn't matter if the same mistake happens five or four or seven times, the exact number doesn't matter here. What matters most is that you expect to make mistakes and consider them to be normal and then make the best out of it.

Don't get angry about mistakes

If you get angry about your mistakes and do not allow yourself to make them over and over again as recommended above, learning will be frustrating and slower for you. Being annoyed always means that you put your energy and focus on something that didn't work, rather than acquiring new knowledge and being happy with what you have already accomplished. It is best to be grateful for every mistake you make while learning. If you make the mistake now while learning, you will avoid making it later in an exam or in a professional situation where it could become embarrassing.

Learn the mistakes more intensively

If there are things that you keep getting wrong, check if your memorised picture or story is suitable for you and adjust if necessary. Also, use the reinforcement techniques you learned above. You can change your picture completely or just add more details to the existing picture to make it more vivid. Also, use emotions, add more sensory impressions, and make sure that you yourself or people who are especially important to you are part of the story. In my experience, most of the pictures that did not work well the first time around started working well once I had applied the techniques I just mentioned. So just play around a little bit. The more practice you get with this kind of brain-friendly learning, the easier it will be to create the right images.

How to create long-term memories

One of the aims of this book is to show you how you can store what you have learned in your long-term memory. It is not just about learning something for the next exam or next meeting and then forgetting it. There are a lot of things you need to know long-term, like if you want to learn the vocabulary of a new language or if you want to have the names and background information of customers ready for the next meeting. In these scenarios it is not enough to just be able to remember the items for a few days or a couple of weeks; you need it in the long run—a few months and or even years.

At the same time, you don't want to have to repeat the same material every day, especially if you want to learn a lot of information. If you have learned and used the techniques in this book, you know that rote learning and excessive repetitions are exactly what you want to avoid in the future. This approach leaves something to be desired in terms of only being able to recall bits and pieces of the material in the long run!

Repetitions are definitely an important part of learning. I like to compare it to a meadow that you cross on foot. If you walk across a meadow, you will likely leave a trail through the grass, but by the next day all traces will be gone. That is also the case when we try to remember something without any aids. It remains in our memory for a short moment but is usually forgotten very quickly. Just imagine that someone tells you a short, maybe seven-digit, number. You can just repeat it a few times and then be able to recall it correctly as might be useful when, for example, logging in to a web page that requires a temporary code that was sent to you by SMS as part of their 2-factor verification.

The good news is that there is a procedure that allows you to transfer your learning material into long-term memory without having to repeat it every day. This method is called "interval learning". With interval learning, also known as "spaced repetition", you repeat the learning material at predefined intervals that allow you to transfer the new information into your long-term memory with as little effort as possible:

1st repetition: after one hour maximum
2nd repetition: after one day
3rd repetition: after three days
4th repetition: after one week
5th repetition: after one month
6th repetition: after half a year and then every half year

If you have repeated what you have learned in this way, about 90–95% of the information should actually be retrievable in your long-term memory. This is because your brain has built up the connections among brain cells in such a way that they are available for a long period of time.

By the way, this way of repeating is also helpful and necessary when using the memory techniques described here in this book. When you use the PC and UK methods and create a lot of pictures and stories for what you want to learn, especially if it is a lot in a short time, you do not want to spend too much time repeating them until they stick in your memory. If you stick to the learning intervals introduced above, you will minimise revision time.

To understand this concept better, it is helpful to take a look at the "forgetting curve", which was first described by German psychologist Hermann Ebbinghaus in 1885. He is generally considered to be the founder of modern memory research and has conducted experiments on how long people can remember newly learned information and how quickly we forget things. He found out that already after twenty minutes, only 60% of learned material is retrievable, after one hour only 45%, after one day 34%, after six days only 23% and beyond that only 15%—which ends up being approximately only one out of seven items!

These figures are not absolute, however, as Ebbinghaus used meaningless syllables in his experiments rather than content he was keen on learning. As these syllables were abstract and meaningless, they were fundamentally more difficult for the memory to retain than pictures, stories or comprehensible logical connections, but the general principle still applies.

Forgetting can, as we all know from our own experience, be reduced by repetition and sometimes be avoided altogether. Interestingly, every time you repeat something, the "forgetting curve" flattens out, i.e. it takes longer until we have forgotten 40% of the content, so for the very abstract meaningless syllables the second time round, it might not take twenty minutes anymore but maybe thirty minutes. And the third time even longer. This can also be illustrated using the following graphic:

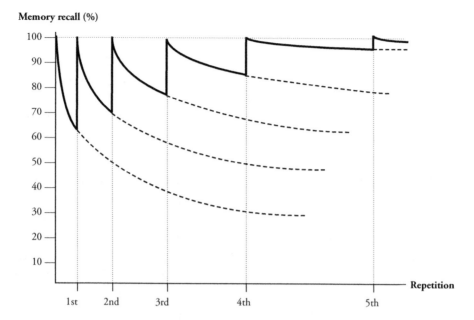

The flattening of the "forgetting curves" after each repetition also increases the necessary time interval between repetitions in order to get back to the upper line, which I call the "knowledge line", with the same effort. Give it a try! Your own experience is the best way for me to convince you that it works!

Summary

Congratulations! You have successfully completed this chapter on the basics of brain-friendly learning. I hope I was able to show you the power of picture-based learning where you create a picture for everything you want to learn and connect this picture to a prepared mental structure that is also picture based. This way, your brain will be able to retain and recall information much more easily and quickly.

You have seen that you can learn a list of items in the right order by creating a story around the items or by attaching the pictures for the learning items to pictures of the prepared mental structure like our body list. When you use a prepared list to learn a list of new items, the advantage is that you can also tell the exact position of the new item in the overall list. While this is not always required like it is for the shopping list, it can be quite useful in many other instances such as the list of chemical elements, a list of arguments you might want to learn for a speech or when learning about laws and regulations.

Another important point covered in this chapter was the method of optimal repetition intervals. This helps you to transfer your learnings from your short-term memory into the long-term memory with the least required effort.

So far with the Body List, you only have ten places available on the list—clearly not enough for many situations. In the next chapter, we will look at ways to create more and longer prepared lists so that you are well prepared for learning projects of any size!

Review questions

1. What is the Body List and how does it help you to memorise a list of items, e.g. a shopping list?
2. Can you still remember the shopping list you learnt in this chapter?
3. What were the methods for strengthening your learning pictures?
4. How do you best deal with mistakes while you are learning? What should you not do? What should you do?
5. What can you do to reduce stress while studying?

CHAPTER 3

LEARNING LISTS

Why learning lists is so important

In the previous chapter, I showed you how easy it is to memorise a shopping list with ten items using the Body List. It was easy to picture a pumpkin, a water bottle and a loaf of bread. Also, the list was short, being comprised of only ten items. If you are a professional and want to develop your skills and knowledge, you will also want to do the following:

- Learn long lists of facts, not just ten items, so you will need longer prepared lists
- Learn from different areas of knowledge, so you will need a variety of different prepared lists
- Learn things that are not as easy to visualise as a pumpkin or a water bottle, things that are likely to be more abstract so you will need strategies to turn abstract concepts into pictures and learn them just as easily as the simpler ones

The good news is that there are solutions for all three challenges, and we will cover them in this chapter. The first point to realise is that there are many more lists in everyday life than it seems. They might not reveal themselves at first glance, but with the right approach, you can turn many things you want to learn into lists and memorise these with the methods presented in this book. I like to separate them into two groups: the obvious lists and the hidden lists.

The obvious lists already come in list form. For example, the answers to certain questions that you might type into Google are inherently lists, such as:

- What are the Seven Wonders of the Ancient World?
- Who were the presidents of the United States (or whichever country you wish to use)?
- What are the ten highest mountains (in the world, in the US, in Europe, in Asia, etc.)?
- What are the Ten Commandments?
- What are the amendments to the US Constitution?
- What models can be used to evaluate the attractiveness of an industry?
- What are the essential and non-essential fatty acids?
- What are the layers of skin?
- What are the seven deadly sins and cardinal virtues?
- What are the assumptions behind the IS-LM model (a standard model in economics)?

You can also turn other things you might want to learn into a list, but these lists may not be immediately obvious:

- Texts of any kind: they contain a series of arguments that you can convert into a list
- Poems: you can convert each row into a picture or brief story and learn their order as a list
- Maps: by establishing a certain journey through a continent or the individual states of a country, you can also learn the location of a country or state as a list

In this chapter, we will therefore learn how to create new standard lists, so you have multiple ones including those of different lengths for variety. To convert your learning content into picture-based lists, we will look at various examples and convert abstract items into pictures.

Building a palace for your memories

A highly effective memory technique that has been around for over 2,500 years was discovered by a well-known ancient Greek statesman and poet named

Simonides of Keos. He earned his living as an entertainer for the banquets that the rich and powerful used to organise back in those days.

The most famous speaker of his time, Cicero, included the following passage, in his book about public speaking *De Oratore* which describes the legend of how Simonides discovered a fundamental and very important memory technique. Here is an excerpt from Wikipedia[1] (translated from German):

> *"At a banquet hosted by a Thessalian nobleman named Skopas, Simonides recited a lyrical poem in honour of his host, which included a passage on the fame of Castor and Pollux. The frugal Skopas told the poet that he would pay him only half of the sum agreed for the praise song, and the rest he should receive from the twin gods to whom he had dedicated half the poem. A little later a message was brought to Simonides that two young men were waiting outside to speak to him. He left the banquet but could not see anyone outside. During his absence, the roof of the banquet hall collapsed, burying Skopas and his guests under its rubble. The corpses were crushed beyond recognition so that the relatives who wanted to collect them for burial could not identify them. But since Simonides remembered how they had sat at the tables he could show the relatives where each of their dead had sat. The invisible visitors, Castor and Pollux, had paid generously for their share of the praise by removing Simonides from the banquet immediately before the collapse".*

We do not know whether this event happened precisely in the way described by Cicero. What is important is that Simonides was able to identify the bodies because he was able to remember where each had been sitting that evening. While he had been on stage, he could see the guests the whole time and afterwards, when he was asked to identify the dead, he could do so by recalling these images in his mind's eye. This is precisely what you do when you apply the PC principle; you create images in your mind that the memory can store easily. When you want to recall the information contained in them, you can easily recall the stored image and translate it back to the information you wanted to remember.

---

[1] https://de.wikipedia.org/wiki/Simonides_von_Keos

In ancient times, when speakers in public places such as the Greek Agora or the Roman Forum made their speeches, which were often very long, they did so with no written notes. There were ways of writing things down, but parchment was very expensive and was not used for something as banal as a speech manuscript. Also, it was considered beneath the orator's dignity to use notes. The speaker would typically learn the speech by heart using a technique called the Method of Loci, using something known as the *memory palace*.

Since the orators always gave their speeches in the same places, the speakers knew these places very well and were familiar with their details. They knew exactly what they were going to see when their gaze wandered across the square. They knew each temple, each statue, each market stall in and out. They could close their eyes and see these images as if they were standing directly on the square.

Try it out for yourself. Close your eyes and put yourself in a place you know very well. Maybe the easiest place to do this with is your apartment or house. Step inside through the front door, leave your keys and jacket where you always leave them, take off your shoes and put them where you always put them. Go through the first door on the left and enter the next room. Now walk through this room in your mind. What is the first thing you see when you look to the left? Let your gaze wander clockwise through the room. It is amazing what your mind's eye can see, isn't it?

What the ancient speakers did was memorise the various objects in the marketplace where they would speak so they could recall them in the right order and recite them one by one. That way, they created a familiar, known structure, and, in keeping with our UK method, to which they could now attach unknown content.

If they wanted to learn a speech by heart, they took their arguments, stories and examples and mentally attached each of them to the various objects in the marketplace. When it became time to actually stand in front of the hundreds or thousands of listeners and deliver their speech, they had to look at or think of the next object, and by connecting it to the picture they had visualised for the argument, they knew exactly what they wanted to say next.

As I mentioned above, this method is called the "Method of Loci". The term "loci" comes from the Latin word "locus", which means "place" because we attach our learning images to known places. You could also say that you are using *memory palaces* because a *memory palace* is an imaginary room where you use objects as hooks to which you attach the items you want to remember. Also, because you walk through this room as if on a journey, it can also be referred to as the "Journey Method". Whatever you want to call it, it is a method that memory champions use to remember immense quantities of information in a short time. The fact that it has endured for over two millennia by now is a sure sign of its effectiveness!

Applying the Method of Loci

In seminars where I am in a room with my audience, I can demonstrate this more easily because we can all see what the room looks like and what objects are in it. It is more difficult to explain using a book, so here is a picture of a room, which I will use in the following example.

If you look at the picture from left to right, you will see the following objects. If you don't have the picture available, it is not a problem; just imagine a room with the following items in a sequence from left to right:

1. lamp
2. painting
3. sofa
4. cushion
5. roses
6. table
7. clock
8. window
9. little wooden man
10. drawer

Take another close look at the picture or go through the ten items in your imagination until you have memorised the order well. This room with its ten items has just become your first *memory palace*! You can now use it to remember more lists. Here is a sample to-do list of ten things you might have to get done in a day and would therefore want to memorise:

1. Take a letter to the post office
2. Have the tyres of your car changed
3. Buy a gift for your child's birthday
4. Submit a request for vacation
5. Order cinema tickets
6. Send a job application
7. Read newspaper article about the new iPhone
8. Get a haircut
9. Order printer cartridge
10. Pick up daughter from kindergarten earlier than usual

How can you now connect the individual activities with the places in the living room we have listed above? Try it for yourself! Practise creating your own connections between the pictures. Below are some ideas on how you can create them:

1. lamp - take a letter to the post office
You go to the post office to post a letter and the mailbox is lit by a huge, dazzling lamp.

2. painting - have car tyres changed

Somebody painted your car tyres in bright colours so you need to have them changed.

3. sofa - buy a gift for a child's birthday

In your living room there is a children's birthday party going on and all the little ones are jumping up and down on your brand new, very expensive sofa surrounded by a sea of gifts.

4. cushion - submitting a request for vacation

You go on vacation to a very nice beach resort where you lie on very comfortable cushions. (The thought of being on vacation should be enough to remind you of the request for vacation.)

5. roses - order cinema tickets

You take your partner to the cinema and upon entering the theatre, you are each handed a beautiful rose.

6. table - send a job application

You imagine how you would sit across the table from an interviewer at a job interview, which you got successfully after sending in your application.

7. clock - read newspaper article about new iPhone

The alarm on your iPhone goes off. You silence it and then open the app for your favourite newspaper and start to read it.

8. window - get a haircut

You look at your reflection in the hairdresser's window as he cuts your hair and you feel your hair getting shorter.

9. little wooden man - order printer cartridge

The little wooden man wants to change the colour of his clothes and pours the contents of a printer cartridge over himself, creating quite a mess.

10. drawer - pick up daughter from kindergarten earlier than usual

You are late in picking up your daughter from kindergarten because you forgot it needed to be earlier, so you take a flying drawer instead of a car for transportation.

Now see how well you can remember the ten to-dos by filling in the spaces in the following list:

lamp _____

painting _____

sofa _____

cushion _____

roses _____

table _____

clock _____

window _____

little wooden man _____

drawer _____

How many of the to-dos were you able to remember? Even if you just got seven of them, that's already quite good. If you got eight or above, you have pretty much already internalized the method.

Did you notice that some of the pictures used above didn't exactly illustrate the task, but only something close to it (e.g. picturing the vacation and not the actual vacation request)? The picture does not have to be exactly the same as what you want to learn, it just has to be similar enough. You are the only one who can decide what is close enough for you! If you realise in future repetitions that you need more details in your pictures or stories, you can always add them later.

How to create your own memory palaces

You have just seen how powerful the Method of Loci is for remembering lists with its *memory palaces*. We used the PC principle, which involves connecting the elements of the *memory palace* with the symbols for the items we wanted to remember. To use this method effectively, it makes sense to use the UK principle—that is, to create a structure with which you are familiar, the prepared structure, and to attach the new, unknown things to it. Your goal should be to prepare several *memory palaces* over time, which you can use in different learning situations and for a variety of learning materials.

The following are practises that I have developed over the years and that have helped me construct an overall list of over 1,000 symbols that I can use flexibly in various learning situations.

Memory palaces have twenty-five or fifty locations

My *memory palaces* are comprised of either twenty-five or fifty locations. This is still a manageable number and sufficient for most learning projects. These numbers are not set in stone. You may create shorter or longer journeys, depending on what works for you. When the actual real-life journey is not long enough or does not yield enough unique items, I go for a shorter list; if there is more variety, I create a list of fifty items.

I also connect the locations with numbers, just like we did with the Body List, so that I can learn ordered lists easily—lists where not only the exact order of the elements is important but also the concrete position of an element in the list. For example, if I want to know the eighth element of the periodic table of chemical elements, not only do I need it to be a place on the journey through the *memory palace,* but there also needs to be a precise number associated with it. The effort it takes to learn may be higher in the beginning, but it pays off later in the concrete learning process in that you can use your *memory palaces* in a more flexible manner.

Memory palaces from everyday life

When I started building my *memory palaces*, the first thing I did in everyday life was look for routes I used regularly. I am spending a lot of time in my office, so I built one *memory palace* in my office. Then I took my regular jogging route; by running it several times a week, I know it very well, and it was easy to learn and repeat it. With that, I already had another hundred storage locations for any new items I wanted to learn.

When you follow this approach, keep looking at the places where you spend time regularly and see if you can turn them into *memory palaces*.

Vacation palaces

Over the last few years, I have been on vacation to the same places several times with my family, so I know each of them well by now. Whenever we were on holiday in a new place (usually for two or three weeks), I would design a *memory palace* for the new place at the beginning of the holiday, usually within the first week, and then give myself a week or even two to internalize it. The advantage of these *memory palaces* is that when the holidays were particularly nice, these places would be emotionally positive for me; this made learning with them beautiful, relaxed and thus even more productive!

Apply and repeat

What applies to all learning content naturally also applies to my own *memory palaces*: to use them, I have to repeat them at the optimal learning intervals. The nice thing is, whenever I use them, I repeat them at the same time! A little tip: if you always use a *memory palace* from the beginning, you will master the beginning very well while you will become less familiar with the places that come later in the list. To avoid this, you can also start in the middle or towards the end to repeat this part. That is one reason it is so useful to separate a *memory palace* into different parts so that you can start at the first element of each room and therefore be more flexible. In the next chapter, you will see how we apply this principle in practise.

You might ask yourself, "Isn't this all a bit confusing?" Usually, it is not. If you want to learn, for example, a list with 18 items, you could start in the fourth section of a five-section list (if you follow my example of creating lists with 50 items), that is, you have the last 20 places of the *memory palace* where you can place the 18 things and thus repeat this part especially. Just try it out. If it works, all the better; if not, don't worry!

As with everything that you have learnt so far in this book, your success will be determined to a large part by your willingness to try, improve and adapt. Some things will flow naturally for you, others will require a bit more practice. The most important thing is not to give up! Very soon the progress you are making will make it all the easier to continue.

Another example of how to apply this technique

The first step is to make sure that what you want to learn is in the form of a list. You can then visualise these lists with all the techniques you have already learned and memorise them with the help of one of the lists you are now familiar with, such as the Body List or your own *memory palace*. In the following sections, you will work through some examples that show how this first step of list creation looks in more detail.

Learning obvious lists: The Seven Wonders of the Ancient World

Let's take the Seven Wonders of the Ancient World as the first concrete example and use the Body List for memorising it. The Seven Wonders of the Ancient World are:

1. Great Pyramids in Egypt
2. Statue of Zeus
3. Temple of Artemis
4. Lighthouse of Alexandria
5. Hanging Gardens of Babylon
6. Colossus of Rhodes
7. Mausoleum of King Mausolus

All we need now is a connection between each respective Wonder of the World and our Body List. These could look like this, for example:

1. There's a **huge pyramid** on each toe of your *foot* - which looks pretty weird. I know that the pyramids are in Egypt, so I don't have to learn that part separately.

2. I already know that **Zeus** was the king of the gods, and as king, he will not *kneel* before anyone; everyone else has to kneel before him. If you have not heard about him before, you could visualise a king holding a glass of juice in his hand ("juice" rhymes with "Zeus").

3. In a temple, a little girl—or a little **miss**—is looking at a piece of **art** that has been placed on her *thighs*. (Here the first part of the word "Artemis", which I would like to turn into a picture, comes before the second in the sentence, but I trust that my brain will remember that there is an inverted order here, especially since I have heard the name in the past. If you don't know the name and want to make sure you don't mix up the order, you could add a small, cute ant (or a big and dangerous one) to the story so you can remember that the goddess's name starts with "A").

4. I hold a **lighthouse** between the cheeks of my *behind* and at its top I can see Cleopatra (here I know that she lived in **Alexandria** as Queen of Egypt).

5. A **baby** with an enormous *belly*, which **hangs** down quite a bit, plays in the **garden** (the "baby" is enough for me to remember Babylon).

6. Here I imagine the broad, muscular *chest* of the **Colossus of Rhodes**, and since I have heard enough of the Colossus of Rhodes, that is enough for me to remember it. If you have never heard about Rhodes, you could imagine that he is so big that he needs to walk on two roads at the same time. Since "roads" sounds exactly like "Rhodes", you have the connection.

7. A **king** has a *mouth* as big as a **grave**, and a cute little **mouse** is running inside of it. You might already know that a mausoleum (whose meaning is actually derived from the grave of King Mausolus) is a special kind of grave. This can also be used as a mnemonic device here.

These are suggestions from me as to how you can remember the Seven Wonders of the Ancient World. And again, there is no right or wrong. The only thing that matters is whether the connection and the story help you and whether you can remember them well. If you have a connection that works better for you, then it is automatically better for you and you should use it!

Learning more complicated things

If you search for the Seven Wonders of the Ancient World on Wikipedia[2], you will find that the Wonders of the World are described here in more detail. I have kept the order from above. On Wikipedia they are arranged differently, but we will discuss why I changed the order later.

1. Great Pyramids of Giza in Egypt
2. Statue of Zeus of Phidias of Olympia
3. Temple of Artemis in Ephesus
4. Lighthouse on the island of Pharos off Alexandria
5. The Hanging Gardens of Semiramis at Babylon
6. Colossus of Rhodes
7. Tomb of King Mausolus II of Halicarnassus

If you want to learn more facts and name extensions about the Wonders of the World now, you can simply add to your existing stories. This makes it more complex, but then you also want to learn more facts. Here are my suggestions for the memory stories:

1. *Great Pyramids of Giza in Egypt:* There's a **huge pyramid** on each toe of your *foot* that looks pretty weird. Next to one of the pyramids you can see Lisa (which rhymes with "Giza"; if you have a friend or at least know a Lisa, then picture that person). I know that the pyramids are in Egypt, so I don't have to learn that separately.
2. *Statue of Zeus of Phidias of Olympia:* I already know that **Zeus** was the king of the gods, and as king, he will not *kneel* before anyone. If you have not heard of him before, you could visualise a king holding a glass of juice in his hand ("juice" rhymes with "Zeus").

---

2   https://en.wikipedia.org/wiki/Wonders_of_the_World

As king, he has many advantages and can always be present at the **Olympic** Games where he meets Spanish **phi**losophers and greets them with "Buenos **días**!".

3. *Temple of Artemis in Ephesus:* In a temple, a little girl—a little **miss**—is looking at a piece of **art**, a painting, that has been placed on her *thighs*. On the painting she sees how a frog (which stands for the letter "F") gets into distress at sea and sends an **SOS.** ("F" and "SOS" are close enough to remind you of "Ephesus".)

4. *Lighthouse on the island of Pharos off Alexandria:* I have a **lighthouse** stuck between my behind and on it stands Cleopatra (here I know that she lived in **Alexandria** as Queen of Egypt) who looks at the **Island** of the **Pharaohs.**

5. *The Hanging Gardens of Semiramis at Babylon:* A **baby** with an enormous *belly*, which **hangs** down quite a bit, plays in the **garden** with half a ram, so that makes it a **semi-ram, is** that not funny?

6. *Colossus of Rhodes:* Same as above.

7. *Tomb of King Mausolus II of Halicarnassus:* A **king** has a *mouth* as big as a **grave**, and a cute little **mouse** is running around in it and playing with a **swan** (the symbol for 2, or "II": the second). On the outside you can hear **rally car**s that were built by **NASA's** engineers and that are being driven by fierce-looking hedgehogs (the symbol for "H" so you remember that it is not "Ralicarnassus" but "Halicarnassus").

This example clearly demonstrates that with this method, it is easy to remember several things like shopping lists or the Seven Wonders of the World by combining a prepared list (here the example used was the Body List) with something new (namely brief stories containing elements that remind you of what you want to learn). It might look like a bit of work putting together these little stories for each item, but with a bit of practice, the overall time you spend learning something new will become significantly shorter. This is because you will avoid the boring repetition of rote learning, therefore making the transfer into long-term memory easier and faster.

Write down the Seven Wonders of the Ancient World to see how well you are able to remember them:

1. _____

2. _____

3. _____

4. _____

5. _____

6. _____

7. _____

If you want or need to learn lists of this kind in the future, I recommend the following concrete procedure:

1. Make a precise list of what you want to learn

In the example above, you can see that there may be a full range of details that are possible to learn about each list item, so it's best to know exactly what you want to learn right from the start. Often these things are already given by the school, university or course materials, but if there is any lack of clarity or you don't have all the details, make sure in the beginning that you really know exactly what you want to learn.

2. Ensure you know the tool you want to learn with by heart

When you learn something new using any standard list, you should never have to revise that list in the process. This is part of your preparation before any specific learning.

3. Find the best order

If the order of the items on a list is not important, arrange the individual elements of the list so you can invent the simplest connection stories. In the two examples above, it was all about having all the things on the list, and the order of items was not important. As I mentioned earlier, I changed the order of the Wonders of the World list compared to the order presented on Wikipedia. I did that to have easier connections to the Body List.

For the statue of Zeus, the knees were an obvious choice to make a connection because, at that time, it was not unusual for people to fall on their knees in front of a king. And also, the broad, muscular chest of the Colossus of Rhodes can easily be visualised. When you have the freedom to choose the order, use it.

4. Create the connecting stories and write them down

Now that you know which part of the known list you want to assign to which new item, you can start creating the stories to connect them. Remember that the more funny, absurd, disgusting or painful the pictures are, the easier it is to remember them! It is also very important to write down these stories because by writing them down, you will already start to learn them.

5. Learn the stories

The most important thing is memorising your stories. It is very helpful to imagine these stories as vividly as possible. When you realise that a certain aspect of the story is difficult to learn, look for an alternative. Often, the first picture or story that comes to mind will work for you but if it does not, change it. You are in charge of your stories!

6. Check how well you remember what you have learned

Now recite or write down the stories and the things you have learned and then re-learn what has not stuck yet. I often find this to be the most enjoyable part because time and again, I am amazed at how many of the items I tried to remember and could already recall by the first repetition. This provides you with the motivation to keep going. Do not worry about the things that did not go well; mistakes at this stage are normal—expect them, embrace them, and learn from them. And then, give it another try.

7. Repeat and practise the stories and their meanings

Usually, you will need a few repetitions to get all the material properly stored in your memory. As you can see from the earlier chapter on how to transfer any learning to your long-term memory, there are standard repetition intervals that help you with this transfer in an efficient and time-saving manner. Apply these intervals for any of the examples in this book and your own learning materials, and you will see that your knowledge will grow significantly over time!

With this approach, you can memorise many lists quickly and easily. Especially remember to schedule the repetitions, as in Step 7, directly in your calendar for content that you want to remember in the long term.

Another approach to creating lists

So far, you have learned different procedures with which you can memorise lists of different types in an easy, fast and sustainable way. Now you can start implementing these methods. Before we turn to the next chapter, I want to give you one more very helpful way of creating prepared lists.

The Animal ABC

A simple yet very effective way to create a new standard list is an alphabet list, where you choose a topic and then select objects from that topic that begin with the letters of the alphabet, one object per letter. A simple and useful category to start with is animals. For each letter of the alphabet, think of one animal that starts with that letter and write it down in a list that you then repeat according to the known procedure of optimal repetition intervals. This will allow you to retrieve the symbols quickly and without much thinking.

A possible Animal ABC list could be:

A	ant
B	bear
C	camel
D	donkey
E	eagle
F	frog
G	giraffe
H	hedgehog
I	impala
J	jellyfish
K	kangaroo
L	lamb
M	mouse
N	newt
O	octopus
P	peacock
Q	quail
R	rattlesnake
S	squirrel
T	tiger
U	urchin
V	vulture
W	whale
X	X-ray fish
Y	yak
Z	zebra

If you would like to replace any of the animals with a different one starting with the same letter, do so. I even encourage you to select your own animals so it really becomes your own list. Children in particular like to select their own favourite animals. This has the advantage that the animals correspond to their own world of thoughts. It is therefore more relevant and catchier for the respective individual.

You can use this list as yet another way to learn new lists. It can also help you distinguish ambiguities in the spelling of a word, such as when learning foreign languages. Just include the particular animal in your story as you have done in previous examples like learning the Seven Wonders of the Ancient World.

This technique is so simple and effective that children can also apply it from as early as first grade onwards. I recently taught this technique to my seven-year-old son who could not remember that you write "bread" with "-ea-" and not just plain "-e-". I suggested to him that he could imagine ants crawling all over the bread. Whenever I ask him now how to write bread, he remembers the ants and always spells the word correctly because he remembers the "a".

The Animal ABC list is another prepared list with twenty-six elements. You can also use the same principle to create ABC lists on other topics such as your garden, famous sites or anything to do with a visit to the doctor. You then write one item from this category after each letter of the alphabet, starting with the corresponding letter. It is very important that you can visualise each item easily. With the letters X and Y, I try to use only one of them, otherwise it is usually too difficult. With every new ABC list you create, you have a new list of twenty-five words each.

On my website at www.masteroflearning.com you will find another example of an ABC list, this time using famous sites like the Golden Gate Bridge and the Eiffel Tower, which you are welcome to use for yourself.

Summary

In this chapter I have emphasised the importance of being able to memorise lists. You will find them more often than you might expect in your daily life. You have seen here how you can create your own standard lists using the Method of Loci and how effective it is to remember things like a to-do list.

Also, with the example of the Seven Wonders of the Ancient World, you could recall different levels of details, showing you how flexible this method is.

In the next chapter, you will use the Method of Loci to create an even bigger list which will help you remember long numbers and enable you to be even more flexible with your standard lists. Also, you will learn how to create a list from a map to learn the countries on that map. As an example, we will learn the countries of South America.

Review questions

1. What are examples of lists that you might want to or need to learn? Go back to the beginning of the chapter and check the examples. Were there any examples that you did not initially think of as a list?
2. How long has the Method of Loci been around? How was it used in its early days?
3. How can you easily create your own, very personal *memory palace* so you can use it for your own learning?
4. What is an ABC list, and how can you create your own?
5. Apart from learning lists, what else can you use it for?

Implementation

1. Following the above example, take a room in your apartment or house and create your own first *memory palace* with ten items.
2. Using your newly created *memory palace*, write down a to-do list of your own using ten things to do and memorise them.
3. Review the Animal ABC List, replace any animals where you prefer to use another animal—perhaps you want to use a penguin instead of a peacock—and decide on your own personal Animal ABC. Then, learn and repeat it using the optimal repetition intervals.
4. If you are learning a foreign language, start using it to remember the spelling of words.
5. Explain how to do this to somebody else. This will also help you remember it.

CHAPTER 4

LEARNING NUMBERS

Now that we have covered some basics of brain-friendly learning in Part 1, let us dive into some concrete techniques that will make learning numbers and unfamiliar words, including the vocabulary of foreign languages, much easier and faster.

Meet the Tower List

In the beginning of this chapter, I would like to invite you to do a little exercise with me. I will list twenty items below and I would like to ask you to remember as many as you can, ideally in the right order. You have forty seconds to do this. Set the timer on your mobile phone to forty seconds and get pen and paper ready. Then look at the list while the timer is running and try to remember as many of the items on the list as you can, ideally in the right order. When the timer has run out, cover the list and write down all the items you can recall. Ready?

tower
swan
traffic light
car
hand
six pack
dwarf

hourglass
cat
bible
soccer player
watch
elevator
heart
tennis racket
teenager
magazine
golf ball
dinner
television
Great!

Now cover the list of items, maybe turn the book upside down and write down all the items you can remember. When you have finished, compare what you have written with the list above and count how many items you got right.

How many items did you remember? Are there over seven? Maybe even more than ten? If you have over ten, your memory is already pretty good, and you may have used some of the techniques from the previous chapters.

Now I will let you in on a little secret that will make it much easier for you to remember these twenty items. I'm going to tell you the structure behind the list because, as we discussed earlier, recognizing and learning structures reduces the effort it takes to learn and therefore makes it easier for you.

The following twenty items are symbols for the numbers 1 through 20.

    1 - tower: a tower looks like a 1
    2 - swan: a swan looks like a 2
    3 - traffic light: a traffic light has three lights
    4 - car: the car has four wheels
    5 - hand: the hand has five fingers
    6 - six-pack: there are six bottles in a six-pack
    7 - dwarf: Snow White and the seven dwarfs
    8 - hourglass: looks like an 8
    9 - cat: the tail of the cat looks like a 9 and a cat is said to have nine lives
    10 - bible: the Ten Commandments are mentioned in the Bible

11 - football: in football there are eleven players per team

12 - watch: the dial of a watch has twelve numbers on it

13 - elevator: due to superstition, some hotels do not have a thirteenth floor, so there is no button for it in the elevators

14 - heart: February 14 is Valentine's Day, a day of love symbolised by a heart

15 - tennis: in tennis you count in steps of fifteen: 0, 15, 30

16 - teenagers: there is a famous song "Sweet Little Sixteen"

17 - magazine: there is a magazine called "Seventeen" in the US

18 - golf: in golf you play eighteen holes

19 - dinner: we eat dinner at 7 p.m. which is 1900 hours

20 - television: at 8 p.m. (2000 hours) there is the news on television in most countries

So, now you have logical explanations for the connections of the numbers from 1 to 20 and the corresponding symbols. Cover the list again and write down the symbols once more. How many did you get now? Over fifteen? Maybe even eighteen, nineteen or even all twenty? If there are still a few that did not immediately come to you, don't worry. You probably have made some nice progress. If there are numbers for which you did not remember the symbols immediately, it probably has to do with a lack of familiarity with the concept behind it. If you have never played tennis or never been interested in golf, you might not make the connection between 15 and tennis or 18 and golf. This is not a problem, it just explains why others might get more symbols right this time around. In my seminars, I see this again and again. I once had a young woman who had never heard of Valentine's Day, so the connection of 14 and the heart meant nothing to her. Once she knew about it, she let her husband know, of course! He now helps her remember the connection every year in February!

For the numbers where the connections might seem difficult, look for a connection that is easier for you and replace it. Whilst I will continue to use the above list in some examples throughout this book, if your personal Tower List differs by one or more numbers, this is not a problem as long as you are aware of this change. What is more important is that you feel comfortable with your own Tower List!

If you want to keep the list exactly as I have presented it above, strengthen the associations between the numbers and symbols that do not initially make sense to you. You can do this by perhaps watching a short tennis match on YouTube to see the counting in action, reading a Wikipedia explanation of golf or learning about the origins of Valentine's Day.

Once you have mastered this list, you can memorise a shopping list that is twice as long, since you now have a standard list with another twenty numbers at your disposal. The first step is, of course, to learn this list well so you really master it. Use the optimal repetition intervals from Chapter 2 in order to achieve this. In addition, I recommend you do the above exercise with somebody else and explain the logic of the symbols to them. This way, you can actively apply your new knowledge, make it more real for yourself and in turn, easier to remember. As a third step, you will use this list in the following exercise. This will strengthen your recall and help you to memorise something more complex like, let's say, the locations of countries on a map.

Use the Tower List to learn a map

In order to learn the location of countries on a map—or within a given country, its regions, states or provinces—you first have to convert the map into a list that you can then learn with the methods you are already familiar with. Let's look at the countries in South America as an example. There are thirteen countries so you need a standard list with at least thirteen elements, and because the Body List is not sufficient, you can also use the Tower List.

The first step is to define the list you want to learn. When you look at the map, the best way to do this is to create a route through South America starting at a logical point (either at the top, bottom or either side) and then numbering them as you go. This journey could look like this: You start in the north in Colombia and then go clockwise through Venezuela, Guyana, Suriname, French Guiana and reach Brazil. From here, you cross Uruguay, then Argentina, Paraguay and Bolivia on your way to Chile. The last two countries you travel through are Peru and Ecuador, where the long trip through South America ends.

This journey would give you the following list. I have already inserted the numbers and their symbols, assuming you would use the Tower List:

- tower: Colombia
- swan: Venezuela
- traffic light: Guyana
- car: Suriname

- hand: French Guiana
- six-pack: Brazil
- dwarf: Uruguay
- hourglass: Argentina
- cat: Paraguay
- bible: Bolivia
- football: Chile
- watch: Peru
- elevator: Ecuador

The next step is to link the elements of the Tower List with the names of the countries according to the PC method and to write down these connecting pictures. I assume that you have heard the names of the countries before so you don't have to learn them as names first; we will only focus on learning the locations of each country through the route we chose on the map.

What was probably new to you in this example was the fact that a map could be turned into a list. As soon as you have done this, you can learn the list just like in the other examples. Create your own pictures for the following thirteen word pairs and their connections; then, enter them here.

tower: Colombia
My connection _____

swan: Venezuela
My connection _____

traffic light: Guyana
My connection _____

car: Suriname
My connection _____

hand: French Guiana
My connection _____

six-pack: Brazil
My connection _____

dwarf: Uruguay
My connection _____

hourglass: Argentina
My connection _____

cat: Paraguay
My connection _____

bible: Bolivia
My connection _____

football: Chile
My connection _____

watch: Peru
My connection _____

elevator: Ecuador
My connection _____

Wonderful! Now you have created the links and should be able to not only display the list of countries in the correct order, but also to find them on the map. If you still have difficulties with certain places, here are some suggestions:

1. tower: Colombia - the *tower* reminds me of a **column** which sounds like Colombia
2. swan: Venezuela - **when** I go to the **zoo**, I see a **whale** next to a *swan*
3. traffic light: Guyana - I see a **guy** standing at a *traffic light*
4. car: Suriname - as I am driving in my *car* somebody calls my **surname**
5. hand: French Guiana - a **French guy** holds a baguette in his *hand*
6. six-pack: Brazil - when I spend a day at the Copa Cabana (**Brazil's** famous beach) I always take a *six-pack* of Coke with me
7. dwarf: Uruguay - this *dwarf* is not my guy, he is **your guy**
8. hourglass: Argentina - a couple, **Arch and Tina**, are fighting over an *hourglass* and it breaks in half with the sand pouring out on the floor
9. cat: Paraguay - a *cat* with a **parachute**
10. bible: Bolivia - before eating from a **bowl** I read the *Bible*

11. football: Chile - the *football* players eat **chili** con carne
12. watch: Peru - I look at my *watch* to see how long I take to eat a **pear**
13. elevator: Ecuador - both start with an "E"; since there are no other countries that start with "E", that is enough

When you want to find the pictures to represent the countries, you can use several approaches:

1. *Find a word that is similar:* when we will discuss how to learn vocabulary, foreign words and names we will get into that some more.
2. *Use symbols:* Sugarloaf Mountain or the Cristo Redentor statue could also have been used to symbolise Brazil. You could have done the same with the Eiffel tower as a symbol for France, as another example.
3. *Use your own experience:* if you have been to any of these countries and have had particular experiences there, you can take these. They might mean nothing to other people but be very personal to you; as long as you are not teaching somebody else, what counts is what works for you.

So now you have learnt to convert a map into a list and then memorised it with these (now quite familiar) techniques. You have also practised the Tower List which will come in handy when remembering long numbers.

Remembering numbers

What is the next step to being able to remember numbers with the help of the Tower List and the Body List? First, we have to put the two lists together; otherwise, you would have two symbols for each number from one to ten, which wouldn't help us at all. Since some symbols from the Tower List are based on their similarity to the numbers, we will place the Body List after the Tower List. Our new complete list should then be comprised of the Tower List for numbers 1 through 20 and the Body List for numbers 21 through 30. If you are looking for the symbol for 23, it is the thigh, the chest for 26 and 30 is the hair. For the first half of the Tower List, i.e. the numbers 1 through 9, we will use a slightly different notation. We will write them as two-digit numbers, i.e. "01" instead of just "1", "02" instead of "2" and so on.

So, the new complete list, which covers the numbers from 01 to 30, looks like this:

01 - tower
02 - swan
03 - traffic light
04 - car
05 - hand
06 - six-pack
07 - dwarf
08 - hourglass
09 - cat
10 - bible
11 - football
12 - watch
13 - elevator
14 - heart
15 - tennis
16 - teenagers
17 - magazine
18 - golf
19 - dinner
20 - television
21 - foot
22 - knee
23 - thigh
24 - behind
25 - belly
26 - chest
27 - mouth
28 - nose
29 - eyes
30 - hair

So, now you have symbols for the numbers from 01 to 30 and you can use them to remember long numbers. I will show you how this works with the following example.

Let's say you want to remember the following twenty-digit number:

14291130051301281612

At first glance, there are twenty numbers randomly strung together. Let's display the numbers in groups of two so you get ten two-digit numbers:

14 29 11 30 05 13 01 28 16 12

Next, add the symbols to each of the two-digit numbers:

14 - heart
29 - eyes
11 - football
30 - hair
05 - hand
13 - elevator
01 - tower
28 - nose
16 - teenager
12 - watch

The last step in learning the number is to create a story out of these ten items. First, a practical hint: the symbols of the numbers are clearly defined here, i.e. 14 stands for the heart, 29 for the eyes, etc. In practical use, however, I allow myself a certain flexibility in translating the numbers to the symbols in order to have more creative freedom when creating the stories. The heart is also a symbol for love and therefore I often use the verb "to love" in a story when I want to illustrate the 14. And since loving is an emotion, it also helps with learning. I also do this with number 11 (football), where I use both the ball and the football player or, more rarely, the football field. The same applies to tennis and golf. Also, you can use watch and clock interchangeably since the logic applies to both equally, only that one is bigger. Finally, mouth, nose and eyes can also represent what I do with them, namely eat or taste, smell and see.

Let's go back to the story that I wrote from my own perspective so it is easier to imagine everything in my mind and above all to make the sensory impressions more intense:

> *I love to see when football players have long hair that I can touch with my hand. It makes me feel like I'm in an elevator that goes up a tower to a viewing platform where I can breathe in fresh air with my nose. There are already some teenagers standing there in front of a gigantic clock.*

Now let the story unfold slowly in front of your inner eye. Focus on each number symbol intensely. The love you feel when seeing long hair, the football player with the extra-long hair, the feeling of running your fingers through it with your hand, the acceleration as the elevator rises up the tower, how you step on the platform and take a breath of fresh air, and then the sight of a couple of teenagers standing in front of a huge clock.

You'll notice that I've added details in a few places to make the story more concrete in order to remember the image more easily. If you want to add other details or create your own story, that's better anyway because then it corresponds to your experiences and your personal pictures. If it helps you personally, it is what is right for you!

After you have played the story two or three times for your inner eye, put the book aside and play it again, but this time with the focus on the number symbols. You love the sight of long hair; this represents first the heart, then the eyes and then the hair, which translates to the numbers 14, 29 and 30. Footballers often have long hair that you would like to touch with your hand, so this would be 11 and 05. Then the elevator that takes you up to the top of the tower where you take a deep breath through your nose, so this means 13, 01 and 28. And finally, the teenagers standing in front of the clock signify the numbers 16 and 12.

I have already emphasized several times that brain-friendly learning is a very personal matter. The basic techniques are the same for everyone, but the ones that work especially well for you and how you apply them through the pictures and stories you create for yourself to learn depends very much on your experiences, your previous knowledge and your personal situation. It is always better to create your own story.

Take another look at the numbers and their corresponding symbols and create your own story with which you can remember these numbers. It is best to write the story down. This is often very helpful the first time. The second time, visualise it and go through it step by step. Finally, write down the numbers in the correct order by going through the story again, paying special attention to the number symbols and then translating them back into numbers. In doing this, you should be able to write this twenty-digit number down quickly and correctly.

It even works backwards!

The nice thing about this technique is that with some practice you should be able to write the number backwards! Just think about the end of the story. There were the young people who are standing in front of the clock (I'll take my story again as an example). The young people came before the clock, so when you recite it backwards, the clock must come before the young people. The clock is the 12, the young people the 16, so it would be 12 16, except now you have to turn the two-digit numbers around, so the 12 becomes 21 and the 16 becomes 61, so the number starts backwards with 2 1 6 1. Before the young people standing in front of the clock came the ride in the elevator up to the tower where I took a deep breath of air through my nose on the observation deck. If I turn this around now, the order of the symbols becomes nose - tower - elevator, so 28 - 01 - 13 or backwards it is 8 2 1 0 3 1.

If reciting the number backwards seems too difficult at first, do not get hung up on it. Just do the same for the rest of the number and you will have written or recited the entire number backwards. Practise remembering the number in its original order first. You can then try reciting it backwards again, but the primary focus should be on remembering the original number.

You will probably rarely find yourself in a situation where you have to recite the number backwards; however, it is a cool trick that is not very difficult to learn and makes a big impression on people who are not familiar with this way of memorising numbers. In situations that require you to demonstrate what you are capable of—as in a job interview—this new ability might come in handy. I have been told about cases where this was a deciding factor for similarly qualified candidates. It's definitely something that sets you apart from other candidates!

Here are some more twenty-and thirty-digit numbers with which you can try this technique further. I made sure that only the two-digit numbers from 01 to 30 were used.

3 0 0 7 1 4 1 1 2 3 2 2 2 0 2 7 1 9 2 5

0 8 1 3 0 3 0 1 2 2 3 0 1 5 0 4 1 5 2 9

2 9 2 6 0 9 0 5 2 6 1 6 1 5 0 5 1 8 1 3

2 1 0 1 1 9 0 4 0 2 1 5 1 7 0 3 2 8 1 6 1 4 1 0 0 8 2 5 1 8

0 1 1 5 1 9 2 0 1 6 2 2 1 7 0 6 2 3 0 2 1 7 0 7 1 2 0 6 1 4

1 7 2 9 2 7 1 9 1 4 1 0 2 4 2 8 0 3 0 3 1 2 1 4 0 3 1 6 1 5

Wonderful! Now you understand the basics of learning numbers:

1. Group the number into two-digit numbers.
2. Convert each two-digit number into the corresponding symbol.
3. Create a memory story with these symbols.
4. Learn the story.
5. To recall the number, recount the story and translate each symbol back to its number equivalent.

There is only one problem: you only have symbols for the numbers from 01 to 30. So, now I will show you how to cover the remaining seventy numbers.

Create a list of symbols for the next seventy numbers

In order to cover the next seventy numbers, you must first select seven rooms that you are very familiar with. It is best to select rooms in your house or apartment such as the kitchen, bathroom, living room and bedroom. It could also be your office at work if you go there every day. Or your garden, the guest room, even a storage room. Your car or motorcycle is just as suitable. If you did the implementation exercise in the last chapter, include the room(s) you used there in your list.

My students sometimes ask me what to do if they don't have a garden and only a small apartment. I tell them to use their parents' house, from which they probably moved out of not too long ago. If you have a close friend and you spend a good deal of time at their house, you may select one or more rooms from that house.

Alternatively, you can choose other places that you are familiar with, such as a local supermarket, hospital, cinema or church. The important thing is that you are familiar with it and can easily picture the place in your mind.

In the next step, you put these seven rooms into a specific order. An example could look like this:

3 car
4 living room
5 bedroom
6 bathroom
7 office
8 kitchen
9 garden

You may have noticed that I have written the numbers from three to nine before each room. This is because now specific parts of the car will be numbers 31 through 40, the parts of the living room shall be the numbers 41 through 50, and so on.

Once you have decided on the order of the items, the second step is to choose ten items in each room. The best way to do this is to stand in the main entrance of the corresponding room and go clockwise through the room and select the items. You then use these to illustrate the numbers in this block of ten items.

Let's start in the car. Let's assume that the things you have chosen are:

31 bumper
32 bonnet
33 windscreen wiper
34 windscreen

35 steering wheel
36 radio
37 gearshift
38 horn
39 glove compartment
40 trunk

As you can see, I have written the correct numbers for this numerical block directly before each object. Now I want to cover the numbers 31 to 100 with this technique and thus complete a list with the symbols for the numbers 01 to 100. Going forward, I will refer to this complete list as the "List of 100".

At www.masteroflearning.com you can download an Excel file in which you can enter your rooms and place the corresponding objects in front of their numbers so you have a nice overview of your List of 100. As a bonus, there is also a free learning tool for you as my reader with which you can practise these numbers. Just have a look at it and try it out! There is also a video showing you how to use this tool.

There are a few things to keep in mind when choosing the items in each room. Here are a few more hints before we continue:

- Don't take the same or similar things twice: if you have chairs in the kitchen and living room, choose the chair in only one of the rooms. Even if the chairs look completely different, there is still a chance that in a future story you remember the chair but not the differences that set each chair apart. I'm sure there are enough other items to choose from so it doesn't have to be the same item twice.
- The items should not be too small or even slightly hidden; each should be clearly visible when you look around the room. By choosing rooms that are very familiar to you and that you will continue to use regularly in the future, you will be constantly reminded of the number this item represents. When you are making or having dinner in the kitchen, for example, you can look around and briefly go through the kitchen items and repeat the ten number symbols in your mind. In this way, you will be able to recall the numbers more and more easily over time. This practice requires objects that you can see clearly.
- It's best to choose items that are unlikely to change over time. In the place where the refrigerator is today, there will still be a refrigerator in

the future—even if the current one breaks down. Or you may replace the living room table at some point, but it will probably still be in the same spot. Of course, you will master all the items on your list at some point, but if you use this complete list to learn longer lists by heart, you can easily repeat them whenever you are in the corresponding room. If items should disappear over time, for example, if you have used a child's room where changes will probably occur as the child grows, it wouldn't be so bad since you would likely know the list very well by the time the next change takes place.

For this exercise, we have already illustrated the numbers up to 40. These are just examples, so you should use your own rooms. Even for the numbers from 31 to 40 you should not necessarily use the items listed above but the items from your own room. Below I have listed the other rooms as examples in case this process is a bit tricky for you and thus provided you with a list for the numbers from 41 to 100.

Now let's look at the numbers from 41 to 50, which we will place in the living room as an example. The list could look as follows:

41 bookcase
42 painting on the wall
43 plates
44 windowsill
45 garden door
46 sofa
47 cushion
48 floor lamp
49 stereo system
50 children's photo

The next rooms might look this:

Bedroom:
51 bed
52 blanket
53 pillows
54 wardrobe

55 carpet
56 mirror
57 night lamp
58 window
59 curtains
60 bathrobe

Bathroom:

61 towel
62 bathtub
63 faucet
64 toothbrush
65 shaving cream
66 toilet
67 toilet paper
68 heating
69 dental floss
70 comb

Office:
71 desk
72 monitor
73 mouse
74 keyboard
75 pen
76 ruler
77 whiteboard
78 writing pad
79 books
80 wastepaper basket

Kitchen:
81 light switch
82 calendar on the wall
83 kitchen chair
84 sink
85 stove

86 knives
87 coffee maker
88 salt shaker
89 refrigerator
90 oven

Garden:
91 flower
92 swimming pool
93 firewood
94 fence
95 sun umbrella
96 barbecue
97 bucket
98 shovel
99 ball
100 swing

Now you have filled all the rooms completely and selected symbols for the numbers from 31 to 100. When I want to refer especially to the first twenty numbers, I call it the Tower List. There are other methods to creating a List of 100, but as described above, this method has the advantage that you can practise it daily at home since you have selected the rooms you have in your living space in real life.

This List of 100 is not just a means for turning numbers into pictures but can also serve as a new standard list for memorising longer lists. Think of the possibilities—you can now learn anything that you want!

Start practising the List of 100 directly over the course of the next few days. Begin by downloading the practice tool at www.masteroflearning.com and practise enough so that when you see a two-digit number, you immediately think of the corresponding symbol. Usually it takes a few days until you know the list by heart. Until you really get to the point where the numbers appear in front of your mind's eye without much thinking when you see the item in the room, you should practise for at least five minutes daily. From experience, I can tell you it usually takes about three weeks—and it doesn't really take that much effort. The total amount of time it takes is roughly only the length of an entire movie. Taking the time to do it will help you exponentially when it comes to learning any numbers you might need to learn in the future.

As soon as you are reasonably familiar with the List of 100, start remembering longer numbers. You don't have to limit yourself to using only the two-digit numbers up to 30. Start with shorter numbers, maybe a few numbers with twenty digits, and then go on and on until you can even memorise a fifty-digit number. You will be amazed to see how quickly you can make progress here if you do this once a day and increase the length of your numbers every couple of days!

Summary

In this chapter, I have introduced the Tower List to you, and you have applied it to learning the countries of South America. I have also shown you how you can create your own List of 100. If you do not want to go through the effort of creating your own, just use the one I have provided. Just remember to practise—ideally daily—so you become fluent in the translation of numbers into their symbols. Going forward, this will make it easier to learn lists, especially longer ones, and even more so numbers.

We have done a sufficient amount of work in learning lists and numbers. Now for the next two chapters, let's focus on learning unfamiliar words and as a special treat—finally being able to learn people's names!

Review questions

1. What is the Tower List and how can you link the numbers and their symbols logically?
2. How does the Journey Method from the last chapter help create your own List of 100?
3. How do you convert a map into a list?

Implementation

1. Decide if you want to create your own List of 100 or use the one provided in this book. If you create your own, decide on the rooms you will use and then, one by one, following the instructions above, create the rest of the List of 100 for your own set of rooms.

2. Practise the List of 100 daily for the next three weeks at least five minutes per day so that the translation from number to symbol becomes automatic. Do not forget to download the free practice tool at www.masteroflearning.com.

3. Take any map and apply the approach used above to learn the countries or individual states within a country.

4. Write down any twenty-digit number and practise memorising it—ideally at least once every day.

5. Also try to quote it backwards; this will further strengthen your mental capabilities.

CHAPTER 5

LEARNING NEW WORDS

Introduction to vocabulary learning

Most of us were probably given the opportunity to learn foreign languages in school, especially Spanish or French, although for many pupils it was not an opportunity but rather a painful requirement. I have seen it again and again with classmates and also with friends and relatives that they did not particularly enjoy learning the vocabulary; it was more like torture for them.

We live in a highly globalized world, where the exchange across national borders is enormously important for national economies in general, but also for many of us who are professionally involved with foreign countries. Anyone whose native language is English has, of course, the advantage that most people nowadays speak English, so there is less of a need to learn a foreign language than for, let's say, a Dutch person or somebody from Romania. But even if you are a native English speaker, being able to speak another language well enough for business conversations is often an added benefit and can be very helpful for your career!

When I was at school, I had some initial difficulty learning my foreign languages. Somehow, I still managed to get acceptable grades, but I remember that I also had problems remembering vocabulary for a long time. At that time, I didn't know the techniques that I will introduce to you in a moment.

I remember how I studied the Latin vocabulary of the latest lesson with my best friend one afternoon. There were maybe thirty words and at the end of the afternoon, after two to three hours of continuous learning, mutual quizzing and step-by-step improvements, we were finally able to master the vocabulary. The vocabulary test the next day was very successful, but the words were gone very quickly afterwards. And it continued in this way for a very long time: good memory in the short term, but quickly forgotten afterwards!

Wouldn't it be nice if there were a much faster, easier and more sustainable way of learning vocabulary or any other unknown words for that matter? The good news is that it exists. You have already learnt about the optimal repetition intervals, and these apply to vocabulary as well, of course. But what about a brain-friendly way of turning words into pictures to remember them better?

I have introduced the PC method at the beginning of the book. After all, brain-friendly learning is all about picture-based learning. The best way to do this is to combine the images from a familiar structure such as the Tower List with the images that symbolize the new content, or by stringing images together like a chain and turning them into a story. In these ways, you can easily memorise a shopping list, the countries of South America or the chemical elements. When learning vocabulary, we also use the creative power of visualisation by connecting the images that represent the new vocabulary with the images that represent the meaning of the word. In doing so, it is important to consider how each word differs in terms of difficulty since each level of difficulty requires a different approach.

Level 1: Same words

Sometimes we are lucky and a certain word in a foreign language is the same word as our English one, or at least very similar. Here are some examples:

- die Organisation (German) - the organisation
- l'organisation (French) - the organisation
- el mango (Spanish) - the mango
- die Kreatur (German) - the creature
- la creature (French) - the creature
- la natura (Italian) - nature

There are also words that are basically the same as the English words but have a different ending. These endings follow a pattern and are the same for a wide variety of words; for example, many Italian translations of English words that end in "-ation" end in "-azzione" with the rest of the word being the same. The same applies to many Spanish words, often even the same ones. Learning these words is therefore also very easy as the following translation for "organisation" shows:

- l'organizzazione (Italian)
- la organización (Spanish)

And "motivation" follows the same pattern, and many more words ending in "-ation" in English:

- la motivazione (Italian)
- la motivación (Spanish)

There is a whole range of vocabulary in French, Spanish and Italian which is very similar to the corresponding English words; for example, the words for "important" are very similar in each of the following languages:

- important (French)
- importante (Spanish)
- importante (Italian)

Another example would be the translations of "attention":

- l'attention (French)
- la atención (Spanish)
- l'attenzione (Italian)

When you already know a foreign language and want to learn another one, maybe the new language has words similar in your first foreign language but not in your mother tongue. If you know French and the French word for late ("tard"), you can use this connection to remember more easily that in Spanish "la tarde" means late afternoon and evening, since this is the later part of the day. Or if you know Spanish for "shield" (el escudo), it is easy to remember the Italian version which is "lo scudo".

These words are the easiest to learn and remember, so let's look at some more complicated cases and find out how you can remember these easily, too.

Level 2: New word sounds like another word - The Keyword Method

Even though there are some words that are as easy to learn as in the first level, this is of course not the case for most words. Most of them are not identical or similar. The next level of difficulty are words that sound the same or similar to another word you already know but have a completely different meaning. This other word can come from English or from any other language you know. The most important thing is that you know what it means and can visualise it well. When you have another word that sounds similar to the word you are trying to remember, it does not have to be precisely the same. Remember that our brains are quite capable of making a connection when there is enough of a similarity.

If there is a similarity between a word you know and the word you are learning, you can use the PC method again. To do so, create a picture for the word and its meaning. Then, connect these two pictures in the manner that you are familiar with by now after working through this book thus far. Here are a few examples:

- die Frau (German for "woman" or "wife") - the **woman** is always **frow**ning
- saber (Spanish for "to know"): I **know** how to use a **saber**
- le père (French for "father"): my **father** is biting into a juicy **pear**
- el sol (Spanish for "sun"): the **sun** has burnt the **sole** of my foot
- il pollo (Italian for "chicken"): I play **polo** on a **chicken** instead of on a horse

You can see that the word we use as a keyword does not have to be exactly the same, though sometimes it can be, and might be slightly longer or even shorter.

Sound easy? It is! Once you have created the connection between pictures here, you will be able to memorise the Level 2 vocabulary easily. This method is called the Keyword Method because you find a word you already know as a keyword, some sort of reference point, for the word you want to learn. In a way, the keyword provides the key to the meaning of the new word.

It does not matter which language the keyword comes from for this approach to work. The important thing is, again, that it works for you! So, if you are good at French and you want to learn Spanish vocabulary, use French words that sound similar to the Spanish word. And you can use a word from the same foreign language just as well. As you can see, the more you know, the easier it is to learn new things!

Here is a word of warning: in language learning, there are not only the above examples of words which are the same or similar and therefore easy to learn, but there are also the so-called *false friends*. These are words that are very similar or even the same as an English word but have a completely different meaning. The English word "ambulance" translates to "Krankenwagen" in German, while the German word "Ambulanz" means "outpatient clinic". Or "brand" would be "die Marke" in German, while "der Brand" means "fire".

You have to learn these *false friends* more thoroughly in order not to be tricked by the similarity to the word in the foreign language. And at the same time, the similarities also make learning these words easier by providing keywords you can use to memorise them. Here are a few more examples:

Spanish:
- la firma - signature; the firm - la empresa
- el éxito - success; exit - la salida
- el vaso - glass; vase - el florero

Italian:
- la delusione - disappointment; delusion - l'illusione
- eventualmente - possibly; eventually - finalemente
- la fattoria - farm; factory - la fabbrica

German:
- die Dose - can (container holding liquids); dose - die Dosis
- brav - well-behaved; brave - tapfer
- das Gift - poison; gift - die Begabung

French:
- la chance - luck; chance - la possibilité
- rester - to stay; to rest - se reposer
- la librairie - bookshop; library - la bibliothèque

Step 3: Splitting words into parts and finding similar words for the parts

The third level of difficulty in learning vocabulary includes the most common words in a language. The PC method is great for creating mnemonics that make learning vocabulary easier for the brain. To do this, just divide the new word into parts and then look for similar words, just as you did with the Keyword Method, and then connect it with a picture for the meaning of the new word in a brief story.

To find the best way to break the word into parts, say the word out loud and see which associations immediately come to mind.

mushroom - le champignon (French)

If you break down the word into "champion" and "yawn" you could picture a champion (using only the abbreviation "*champ*"), maybe a boxer who has just won the world title and when he sees his food, some *mushrooms*, he is bored and *yawns*

cat - il gatto (Italian)

By splitting gatto into "gat" and "to" you could remember that you have *got to* find your *cat*

bean - le haricot (French)

You could divide the French word into "hari" and "cot" and imagine that the hair on your *hairy co*at is made of millions of *beans*

bag - la bolsa (Spanish)

When bolsa becomes "bol" and "sa" you can use a ball (here the dancing event) and the beginning of the word "Saturday" to picture the tickets for the *ball* on *Sa*turday that are in your *bag* *dinner - jantar (Portuguese, pronounced "john-tar")*

Here the memory picture could be ***John*** eating **tar** for ***dinner*** (the John could be any John you know, like John Travolta or John Lennon)

As you can see from the examples above, this method works with different languages. Here are some hints for the concrete application:

1. The parts can either be the single syllables that make up the word or several syllables together. It is only important that you can find keywords for the individual parts, which will then be linked to the memory story.
2. You can either encode each part of the foreign word with another complete word or make each part only correspond to the first syllable or syllables of the keyword. For the translation of mushroom above, we used the whole word "champion", whereas we only needed the first part of Saturday, Sa-, for the Spanish bag.
3. It is easier to have the words in the correct order. Their meanings should either be at the very beginning or at the very end and then the keywords after or before respectively. Once you have some practice with this method, you can mix them if it helps you to create a story more easily. The more practice you get with this method, the more flexible the use of the words will be.
4. Again, just as with the Keyword Method in Level 2, you can take the keywords from different languages. When you have enough practice, you can mix the languages. It is basically about creating anchor points that give your memory the right associations to cause it to remember the desired syllable or word part.

Now it is your turn. Read through the examples above once more and see these images vividly in your mind. Once you have done this, write down the meaning of each word below:

woman (German): _____

father (French): _____

dinner (Portuguese): _____

cat (Italian): _____

bean (French): _____

bag (Spanish): _____

mushroom (French): _____

sun (Spanish): _____

How easy was it now to remember these words using the pictures? My students are always amazed at how easy it is once they have experienced the power of the Keyword Method. If you have always wanted to learn a new language in the past but have felt discouraged by the process of learning the vocabulary, try it again now. The approaches described above will make learning any vocabulary much faster.

General tips

Now that we have climbed the three levels of vocabulary learning, I would like to conclude this chapter with some general tips for learning unknown words. These refer to learning vocabulary in general but will also be helpful in the next chapters.

Similar enough is sufficient as long as it works for you

Especially in the beginning, it is not so easy to always find keywords that fit the word parts exactly. The good news is you don't have to. Our brain, with its highly developed ability to associate, is quite capable of linking similar terms without them having to be exactly the same! This makes it much easier for you to create matching pictures as you have much more flexibility than if the pictures always had to fit exactly.

Note the small differences

Especially when you learn several languages, it happens from time to time that words in two (or more) languages are very similar, especially if they have a common origin, like the Romanic languages, which all evolved from Latin. On the one hand, this makes it easier to learn the vocabulary, of course, because you will have new starting points for keywords as soon as you have learned the word in one language. If you can speak Spanish and you know that the Spanish word for cat is "el gato", then you will find it all the easier to learn "il gatto" in Italian. And with a bit of imagination, you can also deduce the French "le chat".

On the other hand, these similarities might lead to confusion about the correct spelling. Have a look at the translations for "family", which are very similar in English, German, French, Italian and Spanish:

the family (English)

die Familie (German)

la famille (French)

la famiglia (Italian)

la familia (Spanish)

Often you don't just want to know the right word and the right pronunciation, but also the correct spelling. When you have words that are very similar to each other, you need to pay particular attention to the differences in spelling. In the example above, note the slight differences between the Italian word and the Spanish one. Both are pronounced the same and spelled approximately the same. In Italian there is an additional "g". This is a place where the Animal ABC could come in handy with a giraffe as the symbol for the letter "g". Now, imagine an Italian family where mommy bakes a delicious pizza and then a giraffe comes to dinner and eats half of the pizza, while the Spanish family sits around a big paella pan, without a giraffe in sight. If you add this little detail to your picture, you will not make any spelling mistakes in either Spanish or Italian.

Foreign words

In almost all languages there are words that have been taken from other languages, often slightly adapted and over time integrated into the language. With some of them, we are probably no longer aware that they are foreign words. Did you know that some linguists estimate that up to 80% of the words in the English vocabulary have been adopted from other languages? These are mostly Latin, Greek and French, but overall more than three hundred languages might be involved.

When you go to a restaurant or a café and know a bit of French, the origin of the words seems obvious. But did you know that *admiral* and *candy* come from Arabic and *shampoo* and *pyjamas* come from Hindi?

The procedure for learning foreign words is very similar, if not identical, to the procedure we have just learned for vocabulary. You use the PC principle here as well, by turning both the foreign word and its meaning into pictures using the keyword method and then connecting these images. Let's assume that you want to remember "to extol", which means to praise. When you hear the words and look for useful parts, you can divide it into "eggs" and "toll" as in tollbooth. So, imagine a large group of eggs driving through a tollbooth and afterwards being praised for this by the people watching who are cheering and clapping.

Regarding foreign words, here is an additional tip: often, people who use more foreign words than the average person appear more intelligent and confident. They are therefore more likely to be taken seriously by others and can be found more often in leadership roles, whether formal or informal. This is true as long as they do not overdo it. You can significantly improve your influence and achieve more success by learning a few additional foreign words. On my website at www.masteroflearning.com you can download a list of common foreign words with their meaning. Just have a look through them, see which ones you know, and learn some you don't know yet. When you use them regularly, over time you will probably notice that people pay more attention to you because you come across as more competent, credible and convincing.

Abstract words

Up until now, we have used mostly concrete items in the examples, such as a shopping list or activities, which are usually not so difficult to picture. But what about more abstract terms like *noise, freedom* or *human dignity*?

Probably more often than not, you will encounter content that contains abstract terms and concepts. This is likely to be the case with, for example, legal or economic topics, where terms such as *freedom of expression, profit* and *unemployment* may occur.

The Oxford English Dictionary defines "abstract" as "existing in thought or as an idea but not having a physical or concrete existence". Therefore, abstract terms have the disadvantage that, unlike objects, they do not refer to something you can see. They are derived theoretical or imagined constructs that we can only approach through symbols.

Even with abstract content, your goal is to make the content more visual so you can remember it more easily. Since there is by definition no direct image for the abstract terms, find an image that represents the abstract content sufficiently well and then can serve as a reminder for you.

Use the first picture that pops into your head, because it is usually the one that is most relevant for you. Please do not waste your time trying to find a different picture that may (or may not) work better, because you can save yourself the time and effort. Most often it does not really get any better. Do yourself a favour and don't talk to others to compare images. Everyone has very individual previous experiences and knowledge and therefore different pictures. Only if you can't think of a picture at all should you ask someone. Check critically to see if the picture really helps you or not.

First, there are abstract terms for which it is quite easy to picture a concrete situation. Take the word "noise", for example. Although you cannot see the noise itself, there are enough situations in life where you have experienced noise. Just think of a construction site where people work with a jackhammer. Or if you are at a disco, it is usually very loud there as well. Or how about a crying baby? All these situations can be pictured easily, and you have probably experienced them all at least once, so they can serve as your memory picture for "noise".

Or how about "joy"? Can you imagine a small child unwrapping a present for his or her birthday and finding the toy he or she has long wanted? You can easily imagine the expression the child has on her face, together with the overall situation, i.e. the birthday cake in the background, the wrapping paper lying on the floor and the toys. And the bright smile of the child would remind you of joy.

To illustrate abstract terms, look at the word and see which picture comes to your mind first. Often, we have such pictures readily available. It is usually the case that the first picture is the best and the simplest because otherwise your brain would not have shown it to you first. There are, of course, more and less abstract terms. While "noise" and "joy", as you have seen above, are quite easy to imagine concretely, terms like "philosophy", "ethics" or "truth" are more difficult to visualise. If you do not know the term or its exact definition, treat the term as a foreign word and proceed as described in the previous section.

You could imagine a term such as "truth" by picturing Lady Justice, which could also symbolize that the practice of law should be about finding the truth. That's why Lady Justice wears a blindfold and holds the scales in her hand. From an academic point of view, this may not all be correct, but if I associate justice with truth here, it helps me and is therefore right for me. Whether or not it helps you in the same way to remind you of the term "truth", you have to decide for yourself.

If you have difficulties finding a suitable image for an abstract term, try to find out if it is easier to visualise the exact opposite. Then either the context in which you learn it makes it clear that the opposite is actually meant, or you cross out the picture mentally with an imaginary thick red marking and remember that image instead. If you are looking for an image for "freedom", you could either imagine someone being released from prison into freedom or you can imagine a person sitting in a prison looking through the bars of the window with their hands on the bars. The last picture is then the exact opposite of freedom, so you put a big cross over the picture in your mind and then it can be a memory picture for "freedom".

Practice also makes perfect with abstract terms, so look for yourself how well you can do with abstract terms:

Adventure: _____

Misfortune: _____

Intelligence: _____

Happiness: _____

Disgust: _____

Desire: _____

Boredom: _____

Innocence: _____

Here are possible images for the abstract terms:

Adventure: here I think of an adventure playground with lots of exciting play equipment, like a wooden castle and a big ship to board; alternatively: any scene from an Indiana Jones movie

misfortune: after a train accident I see the train cars lying all over the place

intelligence: Albert Einstein comes to mind spontaneously

happiness: cloverleaf as a symbol of happiness

disgust: a bunch of worms that come crawling out of a package of flour and I recoil in disgust

wish: a good fairy who could fulfil my wishes

boredom: children in school sitting on chairs looking bored

idea: a drawn light bulb that lights up, this is used regularly in comics when someone has an idea

Reinforcement through details

Before we move on to the next section, here is a short tip for learning abstract terms. As I mentioned earlier in the section on image enhancement techniques, it can be helpful to add extra detail to an image to make it more concrete, clearer and easier to remember. This is especially true here for abstract terms, since the symbols can often be interpreted in other ways. As in the case of the picture for adventure playground, there is no actual difference between an adventure playground and a "normal" playground in terms of the picture. Maybe I wanted to remember playground and not adventure. If you notice that the image does not translate back very well, and you think more of playground or maybe you don't know what the playground should symbolize, just add more details to the image that all point to adventure. First, you could, as already mentioned elsewhere, add the animal that starts with the same letter as the word you want to remember. That would be the ant for "a" as in adventure. Another idea would be to use the image of Indiana Jones exploring a temple or walking through the jungle to make the concept of adventure even clearer to you.

And if all else fails, you can treat the word like a foreign word and in this case, divide the word in two: "advent" and "chair". Then imagine yourself during advent (symbolised by all the pre-Christmas decorations or maybe an advent calendar) sitting in a comfortable chair eating chocolate!

That's all for learning abstract terms. Now, let's get to the learning of names—another exciting challenge!

Summary

If learning vocabulary has kept you from learning foreign languages in the past, now you hold the key to much easier learning: the Keyword Method. By finding words that sound similar to the word you want to learn, or at least part of the word, you can create brief stories that help you remember the new words and their meaning in a very brain-friendly way.

In this chapter, we also covered abstract terms. They do not represent anything visual in and of themselves, but with the techniques described here, you can nonetheless convert them into a picture or short story.

You have now learnt how to convert even the more abstract things like foreign vocabulary, foreign words and abstract terms into pictures. When you combine this skill with your list memorisation skill, you will be able to tackle anything!

In the next chapter, we will look at one particular version of word learning that people often say they are bad at: names. Do not fear; I have a systematic solution for you here as well.

Review questions

1. What is the Keyword Method and how do you apply it to learning vocabulary?
2. How can you break down vocabulary and learn even those words that seem to be the most complicated?
3. What can you do to visualise abstract words?

Implementation

1. If you are currently learning a foreign language, go to the vocabulary list of your most recent lesson and apply the techniques explained in this chapter.
2. Once you have visualised the unfamiliar words and their meaning and created a little learning story, start the optimal repetition intervals by going through the list once more after one hour and schedule another repetition roughly the same time the next day. Also, schedule all the other repetitions in your calendar.
3. Practise visualising abstract words: either words you need to memorise as part of your professional learning or those from the list you can download from my site.

CHAPTER 6

LEARNING NAMES

A general approach to remembering names

When I ask people in my seminars the areas in which they think they have a particularly poor memory, they often mention remembering people's names. It seems that in the past, they might have experienced situations where they met somebody new and could not remember the person's name soon afterwards. This could be quite embarrassing for them if they see that person again! Either they have to avoid calling that person by name or ask for their name again. Sound familiar? The only thing that saves them is if the other person has also forgotten their name.

Learning names is a very helpful and important skill, especially in a professional environment, not only for salespeople, but for anyone whose professional success is based on building and expanding relationships. This is because those who shine with their good memory by being able to remember names well are seen as competent, credible and convincing. On the other hand, anyone who still has to ask for a person's name at the third meeting does not make a particularly good or trustworthy impression!

Our own name is of particular importance to us humans. Even at the age of four months, babies can distinguish the sound of their own name from the sound of other names. There are even studies that show what positive emotional meaning our own name has for us. In one study, product names were tested and different names were presented to the participants of the study. They were asked to choose which products, and therefore which names, they liked best. The researchers found that the products that sounded similar to the name of the trial participant, that shared several letters with the name of the trial participant or that had the same initials were selected particularly often.

On the other hand, and very unfortunately, in some respects names actually present a particular challenge to our memory. First of all, names are abstract terms which, as we have already seen several times in the previous chapters, are not as easy to learn as objects that can be seen. At the same time, with the right techniques and some practice, you can become a true master in learning names! Many of the approaches that you have learned for memorising vocabulary and foreign words also apply to names, and there are more that we will discuss in detail in the next section.

A few more comments on why many people find it difficult to remember names. First of all, names are often presented verbally, i.e. you meet someone, they introduce themselves and tell you their name. So, you only hear it and do not read it at the same time. If the name is mentioned very quickly or you cannot hear it clearly, you have almost no chance of understanding it correctly, let alone remembering it!

If the environment, like a party, is particularly loud then it is even more difficult for you to understand the name. And if you are distracted by a lot of movement and commotion around you, the name goes in one ear and out the other. So, what can you do to remember names well, despite all these adverse circumstances? In the next section, we will come to the concrete procedure you can use to help you remember names better in any situation.

How to approach learning names

So, how does the learning of names work concretely? I'll start from the typical situation where you meet someone new at a party, a seminar or a meeting and you introduce yourself, maybe even talk to each other briefly. In concrete terms, this means that you enter a room and the other person is already standing there (or vice versa, but this makes no difference as to your approach). So, you walk up to them, extend your hand and say: "Hello, I'm James Miller, pleased to meet you." Usually the other person then replies something similar, only with his name of course.

Step 1: Make sure you have understood the other person's name

If you have not understood the name of the other person clearly, you cannot remember it. Unfortunately, most people do not make sure that they enunciate their own name clearly enough in such a situation that the other person (in this case you) can understand it. This is not your fault and it is perfectly okay to ask the other person nicely to repeat their name! Most people in such a situation don't want to admit that they didn't hear the name. But in doing so, they miss an important opportunity. So, if you ask the other person to repeat their name, you show that you take an interest in it and thus in the person him/herself. Only in this way do you have any chance of remembering the name!

Especially at more formal occasions such as a conference or a fair, you are likely to exchange business cards. This, of course, helps greatly with ensuring that you have understood the name correctly. Especially with foreign names, the pronunciation of the name is not immediately apparent from its spelling. Believe me, with Szczensny as my last name I know what I am talking about. Upon reading or hearing this name, you would definitely have to ask for clarification in order to get the pronunciation right!

Step 2: Repeat the name immediately

Once you have understood the name correctly, you should repeat it directly by saying, for example, "Pleased to meet you, Dr Wallington!" In this way you have inconspicuously and respectfully repeated the name directly and thus practised it. This alone does not mean that you will remember the name forever, but it is better than not repeating it at all.

The most common surnames in the English-speaking world are quite simple names like "Miller", "Smith" or "Baker", but, of course, it also happens from time to time that you meet someone who has a somewhat unusual surname (or even first name). In this case, you might ask where the name comes from and what it means. This way you not only show interest in the other person, which is always a good start for a relationship, but you also talk about the name and repeat it a few more times. This also gives you the opportunity to get more visual impressions of this person, which can help you remember the person and the name later. You might even find out that you have certain things in common, which will help create a connection.

When I introduce myself with my surname "Szczensny" (spoken: "Shensni"), I am often asked where the name comes from or also if the name comes from Poland. I then answer that it is indeed a Polish name, becoming even more precise when I mention that it is from Silesia and that my family moved to the Federal Republic of Germany after the Second World War. Since many families in Germany have a similar background, this common ground builds a connection with the other person.

Step 3: Turn the name into a picture

Now it is important to create a visual representation of the name of the other person, so you have a clear picture that helps you remember the name. To do this, you use the same techniques as you do for learning vocabulary and foreign words, except that there are some special features for first names and surnames, which I will discuss in the next two sections.

Step 4: Picture the other person

When you learn names, you also want to use the PC method to remember the other person and his or her name easily. You already have created the first picture in Step 3, which is the name of the other person. Now you need a picture that will help you remember the person him/herself. To do this, look at the person closely (without staring at them too much, of course!) and see if there is anything that is particularly noticeable about this person and that you could use as an anchor to remember them. This could be features like the ears, nose, birthmarks, eyes, stature, hairstyle, scars, facial shape, mouth or chin, but also clothing, a flashy watch, brooch or necklace can be helpful anchors. The most important thing is that it is a truly outstanding feature that this person does not share with too many other people. With more inconspicuous faces, it can be helpful to find more than one anchor point on the person. The picture becomes a bit more complex, but even this usually does not significantly disturb the process of learning the name. In the next section, we will go through a few examples of this so that you can see how it works in practice.

To make this easier, you can do the following: as you approach someone you don't know but who you think you will introduce yourself to in a moment, start observing this person as soon as you see them. This gives you a little more time to find the visual particularity of that person before you meet them. In my experience, after the introduction, the memory is often busy repeating and visualising the name, so it is useful if you have already found the first picture.

If you haven't found a picture for the person before you hear the name, it is very helpful to listen carefully to what the other person says. This may help you find more things that can serve as memory anchors for that person. It can also be very helpful if you imagine the other person doing activities they are not doing at that moment, especially if they are things they actually like to do. If the person tells you that she likes to fish, picture her in a boat on a lake with a fishing rod in her hand. In this way, you use your creativity and your visual imagination in relation to this person, and because this brain activity takes place in a different part of the brain than the normal memory process, it helps you to remember information about this person more easily.

Step 5: Put the individual pictures together in a story

The next step is to combine the pictures for the name and for the person in a little story, which will help you to think immediately of the name when you see the person and maybe even of some more details from your conversation, which you might have additionally illustrated and added to the story.

When creating and embellishing the story, it is especially important here that you apply the amplification factors from Chapter 2, because you are creating this story in your head while at the same time trying to listen attentively to what the other person is saying. So, the more practised you are, the better it will work, especially with the additional information about the person that goes beyond the mere name.

If your first conversation doesn't take too long, you can—after you've said your goodbyes—continue with your story and repeat it in your head so that you can remember it better. You can also check if you have made it emotional or sensual enough, if you have integrated yourself into the story and if you have used exaggerations and action.

Step 6: Repeat the name

What is generally true for learning is of course also true here: repetition enhances the learning effect, especially if it is done at the right intervals. In the situation described above, in which you get to know a new person and talk to them briefly, you can simply repeat the person's name during the conversation without much additional effort by addressing them by their name. This signals to the other person that you have gone through the trouble of remembering their name. Just make sure that you don't do it too often. Overzealous sales-people overdo it and use the name of the potential customer in almost every sentence. Too much then is exactly that: too much. So, use the name sporad-ically, from time to time, but not too often, which would be rather obtrusive.

You should definitely repeat the name when you say goodbye. A sentence like "Goodbye, Mrs Stahlberg, it was a pleasure to meet you." is very appropri-ate and gives you the opportunity to repeat the name of the person opposite you one last time in that conversation.

If the occasion where you met the other person is an event that lasts a little longer, you can usually repeat the names and faces you have learned within the first repetition interval of one hour, thus achieving a first consolidation. If it's a larger event or celebration, you can look around the room about an hour after you arrive to see if you can see the people you have met again from a distance. You can then briefly repeat the memory story for each person you see and thus strengthen it.

Step 7: Take notes after the initial meeting

It is often helpful to take notes immediately after meeting someone. If you have received a business card from the person you are meeting, this is, of course, very helpful as the name, function and company are already on the card. In case you didn't receive a card, you can also make a new entry on your smartphone and write down the physical characteristics you associate with this new contact. In today's age of the smartphone, you could also ask if you can take a picture to attach to the contact info.

If you have met several people during an event, you can use one of the standard lists such as the Body List or Tower List to memorise the names of all the people you have met that day. Then, if you want to repeat the new names over the next few days or weeks, you can check to make sure that you have forgotten no one.

Last names

With surnames, there are varying levels of difficulty, which make it more or less easy to picture them. Here we will take a look at the various groups that surnames are categorised into.

Professions

If you take a look at the most common surnames in the US or the UK, you will find many names derived from professions that used to be very common. A smith, a baker, a miller, a tailor, a fisherman (abbreviated to "Fisher") all were essential functions in earlier centuries when people were often named after their occupation. Today these make up some of the most common surnames in the English-speaking world. Also, names such as Mayor and Bishop fall into the same category.

Picturing surnames based on job titles is relatively easy, because you just have to imagine how the person you just met does this job. If you have met a Mr Fisher, you can imagine him standing in his fishing boat, pulling in the nets. And you could visualise Emma Smith by imagining her standing in front of an anvil and forging a sword with a hammer.

Concrete descriptions

When the surnames are concrete descriptions or things, they can also be easily visualised. Some of them can be grouped into the following categories:

Animals: Wolf, Bear, Swan, Eagle
Colours: Black, White, Green
Descriptions: Short, Little, Young
Geographic origins: London, Lincoln, Derbyshire
Geographic features: Hill, Forest, Stone, Field, Moore, Wood

Weather: Snow, Thunder, Storm

Patronymic or matronymic (named after father or mother): Johnson, Richardson, Wilson

For each of these terms, it should be quite easy to imagine a corresponding picture which you can then build into the story. Not all of these terms are concrete objects, but you can probably easily imagine a picture for "White" or "Short". And with "Thunder" you could either think of Thor, the God of Thunder, who became quite famous through various movies and who supposedly produces thunder with his hammer. Or you could imagine how you are outside while it is thundering, with dark clouds, rain, lightning and the shock wave when the thunderstorm is very close. Maybe then there is the danger that you think of "lightning" instead of "thunder", but in this case, just use the tiger from the animal alphabet and build it into your story to remember that you want to remember a name that starts with "T".

Similar sounding names

Not all surnames correspond exactly to the concrete terms as mentioned above. All that is necessary for easy memorisation is that you can find something that sounds similar. Our brain does not need a 100% match to remember something. In most cases, a similarity is sufficient. How similar this has to be depends on the concrete learning element and on how well you are already practised. So if you find a term which can be visualised well and which sounds sufficiently similar to the surname you want to learn, you can easily integrate it into your memory history; for example, "Sumner" sounds like summer, so when you picture the person with that surname in a sunny scene, maybe sitting by a pool or at the beach with the sun shining, you have a visualisation for "Sumner".

People you know

Another very helpful way to find pictures for a last name is to take a person you know with the same name and use them as a symbol for that name. You can also use a specific person in a story, which usually makes it quite easy. So, if someone's last name is "Hanks", you could just think of Tom Hanks. Or with "Jolie", you might include Angelina Jolie in your story.

Of course, it doesn't have to be a celebrity. The important thing is that you know this person. So, if you know a Michael Hanks with whom you play football regularly or who is the father of a classmate of your daughter's, you can use him as a picture for the surname "Hanks". Sometimes it is even easier to take a person you know personally, because you have a personal relationship with this person and therefore you have a common history or you know characteristics of this person. You may read something about celebrities from time to time, but surely you know your friends better.

In the end, it doesn't matter which one you choose. Just see which person you can think of first for this last name and use this person for your memory story.

Difficult names (all others)

Not all names are relatively simple cases where the illustration is possible via a term that is quite easy to find. In addition, there are the more complicated names, often also those from other countries and languages, such as Sabatowski, Szczensny, Olluri, Üzgür or Abbondanzieri, and somewhat simpler variants like Menzel, Bertram or Lechner. If you don't know anybody with such a name, you can use the same approach that you have already applied for learning vocabulary. So, you divide the surname into single parts, either single syllables or several connected syllables, and search for a word that sounds similar. You then use this word to illustrate the corresponding part and combine the individual words into a short story.

This means that when you meet Mrs. Bertram, you divide "Bertram" into the syllables "Ber" and "tram" and you could imagine a bear getting into a tram, a kind of streetcar and you are sitting in it yourself. You will probably get quite scared. And for Mr Ostrowski you might use "ost", "row" and "ski". "Ost" could be the short form for ostrich and so you can imagine an ostrich sitting in a rowing boat and wearing skis at the same time and you have a picture for "Ostrowski".

Now, it is up to you to practise visualising some last names. Below is a list of last names. Look at them and using the techniques we just discussed create a mental image or a brief story for each of them that would allow you to visualise the name.

Davis   _____

Bennett   _____

Miller   _____

Price   _____

Shaw   _____

Cook   _____

Simpson   _____

Griffiths   _____

Richardson _____

Stewart   _____

In the next section, we will cover first names.

First names

First names, in contrast to last names, do not usually have a commonly known meaning. For this reason, you will not have an immediate picture available in most cases. On the other hand, since there are less first names that are commonly used, it is easier to prepare and practise.

Names with meaning

While they are not as common, there are still some first names with a certain meaning, but this meaning is usually taken from other languages like ancient Greek or Latin:

Justus - the just (Latin)
Felix - the lucky one (Latin)
Peter/ Petra - from petrus - the rock (Latin)
Leo - the lion (Latin)
Chloe - the green girl (ancient Greek)

Now not all of us are fluent in Latin or ancient Greek and know all these (and the many other) meanings of first names (I certainly do not!). Therefore, we would use different approaches to first names to make them more meaningful.

Similar sounding names

In the vocabulary section, you have already learned the Keyword Method, where you looked for a word or part of a word that sounded similar. This word can be an English word or a word from a foreign language you know. For some first names you can proceed in the same way and use a word that rhymes with or sounds similar to the first name. Here are a few examples:

Robert - robber
Harry - hairy
Jim - gym
Emily - family
Bill - bill (one-dollar bill)
Jerry - cherry
Bruce - bruise
Barry - berry

People you know

Just like with surnames, you can use a person you know as a memory picture, no matter whether this person is a celebrity or a personal acquaintance of yours. You then simply build him or her into your story. If you take a well-known person for both the first name and the surname, it is best to let the person who embodies the first name appear before the person who embodies the surname.

Difficult names (all others)

These are all the first names for which you have not found a name similar to the sound of the name. People with foreign first names fall into this category. Here the process is again the same as we used for vocabulary or with difficult surnames. Since I have already described this in the previous sections, I do not need to repeat it here.

Unusual foreign names

If you are travelling abroad, especially in Africa or Asia, you might encounter names you have never heard before more often than in your home country.

Below I have selected a few typical African names that are particularly sonorous or meaningful, so we can look together at how we can illustrate them, even in such cases that are rather unusual in everyday life.

African girl names

Jamila: jam - il - a
I eat **jam** and get **ill** like an **ant** (symbol for the "a" according to our animal ABC).

Deka:
The name sounds similar to "decker" in double-**decker**, so I take a typical English red double-decker bus

Delilah: Deli - la
It is a **deligh**t to see you **la**ugh.

African boy names

Abayomi: A - bay - omi
A baby **on** a **mit**ten

Abiola: A - bio - la
You study an **an**t in a **bio**logy **lab**.

Chiamaka: Chi - ama - ka
A **chi**mpanzee loves ("**ama**" is Italian and Spanish for "he loves") a **ca**ndle.

Ekon:
Economy, the concrete picture could be a shopping street with many shops

Practising names

Now that you understand how you can significantly improve your ability to remember names, let us do some exercises so you can experience how it all ties together. First, it would be good to practise some complete names, i.e. first and last name together. Below, you will find a list of names. Go through them and find a picture or brief story to remember the names.

Tyler Davis
Dominik Bennett
Alaric Miller
Dane Price
Jeremias Shaw
Alice Cook
Isabel Simpson
Hailey Griffiths
Gabriella Richardson
Alison Stewart

When you have memorised all ten names, complete the missing parts in the list below:

Tyler _____

Dominik _____

_____ Miller

Dane _____

_____ Shaw

Alice _____

_____ Simpson

Hailey _____

_____ Richardson

_____ Stewart

The next step is to combine names and faces. Look at the following ten people and ask yourself: what is striking about their face or general appearance? What makes them different from the others? You can then use this as an anchor for that particular person and include this anchor in your memory story.

1. Robert Hall   2. Sara Thompson   3. Bruce Green   4. Oliver Martin   5. Sandra White

6. Esther Robinson   7. William Hill   8. Emily Behrens   9. Lucas Wood   10. Brooke Hughes

Here are my suggestions:

- Robert Hall: sunken cheeks
- Sara Thompson: braided plait
- Bruce Green: bald head
- Oliver Martin: dark skin
- Sandra White: long, dark hair, coloured yellow and green
- Esther Robinson: ginger hair
- William Hill: smartly dressed with a tie
- Emily Behrens: long, blond hair
- Lucas Wood: dark beard, full hair
- Brooke Hughes: straw hat, looks a bit like Meryl Streep

How do these anchors work for you? If you find something else more striking about that person, you should use that. Now go back to the pictures of the ten people and look at them once again, this time focusing on the anchor. Since your brain is well trained to remember pictures, it will still remember all the other details of the faces, even though you mainly focus on the anchors.

Now you can start creating your memory pictures and stories where you include the pictures that represent the first name, the last name, and the anchor you have just selected. Here are my suggestions:

1. A bank *robber* with *sunken cheeks* enters the *hall* of a bank
2. *Tom* the train and his *son*, who has a long *braided plait*, drive through the *Sahara* desert
3. A man with *green bruises* and a *bald head*
4. James bond eats the *olive* from his *Martini* and suddenly turns *dark*
5. A woman with *long, dark hair* walks through *white sand* with *yellow and green* trees in the back
6. *Robinson* Crusoe with *long, ginger hair* is ("*está*" in Spanish) on a deserted island
7. There is an enormous pile of dollar *bills* ("Bill" short for "William") as high as a *hill* with a *smartly dressed* banker on top
8. A *bear* with *long, blond hair* and his *family* (which rhymes with "Emily") *ends* (this completes the last name) his hibernation
9. *Luke* Skywalker has grown a *dark beard* and still has his *full hair* and fights just with a piece of *wood*

10. *Meryl Streep* stands next to a *huge* (sounds like "Hughes") *book* (rhymes with "Brooke") wearing a *straw hat*

Check how well these pictures work for you and adjust them if you find pictures that are easier to remember for you. Then, go through them once more; visualise them clearly and in as much detail as you can in your mind, ideally also the pictures of the person. Once you feel comfortable with them, look at the pictures again and see how well you can remember the names. Write them below the picture and then check the names on the previous page. Are you surprised by how well it went?

Where do you go from here?

As with all the techniques in the previous chapters, now it is up to you to become proficient in learning names since this, too, requires some practice. As you go through life, walking or driving around, meeting people, seeing different shops, and meeting salespeople (often with a name tag) you will be exposed to names of all kinds: product names, shop names, names of people. Each name is an opportunity to practise visualising a name, even if you have no intention of memorising it. You can also do it with names you already know; it is not always about remembering them but about practising how to turn them into pictures and brief stories.

In order to get going, start small with maybe just five names a day. Keep doing this for one month, ideally increasing the number of names per day gradually, but the most important thing being to practise daily. As you do this, the mental pictures for the names will come more easily and quickly so that after a while it will feel more and more natural to hear or see a name and almost immediately have a picture pop into your mind that can help you remember the name.

Summary

How was that? Are you convinced now that, with a bit of practice, you can learn other people's names with confidence? Now you certainly have the techniques available to do so. You went through the seven steps necessary to learn the name of anybody you meet: from understanding their name, connecting pictures for the name and the person into a little story, and then repeating and writing it down after the meeting.

Learning names has many similarities with learning new vocabulary. Knowing foreign languages is also helpful, since it will make it even easier to find words that sound similar to the names you are trying to learn.

Before we wrap up this book in the next couple of chapters, I would like to share one more way in which these techniques can help your career. Since most people say they have a poor memory for names, they will be all the more impressed if you can remember their name when you have just met them. In certain situations, you may have the list of names of the people attending in advance. When you receive the invitation to a meeting by email and can see the email addresses of the other people, these will often be comprised of their first and last names. For more official events, you might even receive an official attendees' list with the names. And should you be the one organising an event such as a conference or a seminar, you will have the list as well.

In these cases, you can prepare the pictures for the names before the meeting, conference or party. When you then meet each person at the event, all you need to add is the anchor for the person him/herself. Imagine how surprised the other person will be that you have no problem repeating their name, without even having to ask for them to repeat it for you! An excellent start to any relationship!

Review questions

1. What is the very first step to learning a person's name?
2. Why is it important to observe people carefully?
3. What can you do to prepare an event where you will be meeting new people?

Implementation

1. Commit to memorising five names you come across during the day every day for the next thirty days.
2. As you watch any film, the news or a documentary, find an anchor for each person you see that you would use to remember them.

CHAPTER 7

YOUR BODY AS A LEARNING TOOL

The ancient Romans had a proverb that said, "Mens sana in corpore sano". In English, it means "a healthy mind in a healthy body". It was already known 2000 years ago that body and mind are connected, and not only because the head (as the seat of the brain) sits on the rest of the body. For learning, this means that a careful use of the body is important for better learning, be it in terms of nutrition, sleep, exercise or stress. We will now examine these three areas in more detail below.

Exercise

Maybe you know the series "Big Bang Theory", which is about a group of highly intelligent scientists who have their difficulties with life outside the academic world. They represent the classic nerds, whose focus is almost exclusively on their intellectual activities. Physical activities such as sports and regular exercise tend to be at the bottom of their list of priorities. This could almost give the impression that mental performance and physical activity are mutually exclusive; however, the exact opposite is the case!

Sport is also an important activity at many universities and especially at British and US universities, where athletic performance is at least one aspect that can have a positive effect on the selection of students. At English elite universities like Oxford and Cambridge, sports competitions have a high priority.

Sporting and academic achievements are definitely not mutually exclusive; on the contrary, they are closely connected.

In a study from 2009, 1.2 million data records were used to investigate the extent to which the physical and mental performance of those doing military service in Sweden were linked. There was a clear correlation between better intelligence test scores and physical fitness, especially in logical thinking and language comprehension. A plausible explanation could be that the young men who had done a lot of sport and were therefore fit had better heart and lung volumes and that their brains got more oxygen as a result. In addition, the release of hormones such as endorphins, the "happiness hormones", could have had a positive effect on the moods of the men compared to those who were less fit and could have contributed to a reduction in stress. Lower stress levels also support learning (see below).

Another study investigated the effects of one hour more of physical education per week at school on the concentration ability of pupils. The result is also clear here: after sixteen months, the physically active children had a 40% higher ability to concentrate.

Aside from just the general health benefits of regular exercise, the benefit of being able to learn more effectively makes sports activities very important when developing your memory. It doesn't matter what kind of sport you choose; the most important thing is that you exercise regularly for at least half an hour at least three times a week. Even a simple walk is enough. If you find it difficult to spend even that amount of time, check out my free eBook on the easiest way to get sufficient exercise even when you are completely pressed for time. You will find it at www.masteroflearning.com/7min.

Physical movement itself also helps you to learn! It makes a difference whether you just sit at your desk or move around while you study. Through the additional movement, other parts of your body are used and thus more impressions are created in your brain, which in turn strengthens the learning effect. Especially when memorising complete texts verbatim, this is a very helpful method. Actors, for example, move frequently while learning their texts, walking up and down and speaking their texts out loud and with a corresponding body movement so that they set additional memory anchors. Afterwards, on stage or while filming, this makes the recall of the text even easier.

It often happens to me that when repeating my memory stories, I am active with my whole body. I move my eyes and arms, my head in one direction and then in another so that I immerse myself in the story as closely as possible, and these movements are part of the story itself.

Nutrition

In addition to regular exercise and adequate sleep, the right nutrition is important for your body and therefore also for your brain according to the motto "You are what you eat". If you constantly eat junk food with lots of empty calories, you will not only become fat and physically lethargic, but this will also do little for your memory. A person's brain weighs on average about 1,400 g, which is only 2% of the body weight of a person weighing 70 kg. At the same time, however, it consumes about 20% of the body's energy. So, the better you take care of your brain, the better it can work for you!

Without going into too much detail about the scientific background, I can recommend the following foods, which according to nutritionists have a positive effect on your brain performance.

First and foremost, you should make sure that you drink enough fluids. There is a rule of thumb that you should drink 30 ml of fluid per kg of body weight a day, so if you weigh 70 kg, that would be 2.1 litres. But not all liquids are created equal, of course! Still water or unsweetened tea is still best. Coffee is also okay. Juices and soft drinks contain too much sugar and are therefore not beneficial for the body so you should avoid them.

Milk in moderation is also acceptable, especially if you drink it as hot chocolate with dark cocoa powder. Cocoa helps you to be calmer and happier—two effects that you can use very well when learning. Dark chocolate with as high a cocoa content as possible is a nice, delicious learning aid! Nuts like walnuts, almonds and especially cashew nuts go very well with it. I often give my children a few cashew nuts and a few pieces of dark chocolate to take to school or kindergarten so they each have a brain-friendly start to their day.

Other helpful foods include eggs, avocados and blueberries; oils such as walnut oil, olive oil and grapeseed oil; vegetables such as broccoli and fish such as salmon, herring and mackerel. Spices should not be missing, especially turmeric, cinnamon and black pepper. I often drink my coffee in the morning with a pinch of cinnamon, some pepper and turmeric and thus have a good start to the day.

At this point, however, the following should also be mentioned: life does not only consist of striving for optimal nutrition. Don't become miserable in the pursuit of self-optimisation! Therefore, check how you can incorporate the above-mentioned foods into your daily diet without being too dogmatic. It is said that the way to a person's heart is through the stomach, but I like to expand this to "the way to a person's life is through the stomach". I try to make sure that 80% of my food is healthy. This way, I do something for my body *and* my brain and strengthen both in such a way that I can eat the remaining 20% with a clear conscience, even if those things are unhealthy. The joy that comes from this helps me to be more relaxed. Fortunately, the healthy 80% are also things that I enjoy.

Sleep

Wouldn't it be nice if you only had to put a book under your pillow and then could wake up the next morning knowing exactly what the book was about? The eternal dream of learning in your sleep!

Even if it doesn't work as easily as that, sleep still plays a very important role in learning. Above all, sleep is important for transferring learned content into your long-term memory, where the information is available to you not only for a few days, but for a very long time, perhaps even for the rest of your life.

When you sleep, you go through various sleep phases, including deep sleep and the REM phase (REM stands for "rapid eye movement"). These phases are repeated several times throughout the night. If you sleep for eight hours, you usually go through four to seven sleep cycles, each about ninety minutes long.

The brain regions that are especially important for learning are the hippocampus and the cerebral cortex. They are in constant exchange during the processes of learning and the way in which this exchange can take place determines, among other things, how easily and sustainably you can remember new material. After you absorb information in the daytime, neuronal structures will begin to form in the brain at night. When you sleep, these structures are solidified. Based on the available information, the important is separated from the unimportant. This is essential for the efficient functioning of your brain so that your attention is not distracted by unimportant things. The important contents are then reactivated in the hippocampus during sleep. These brain activities are similar to the ones that took place during the day and are responsible for finally storing the contents as long-term memory in the neocortex. This process takes place, depending on the type of information stored, in the deep sleep and REM phases, which are therefore especially important for the consolidation of your knowledge.

Various studies have investigated how important sufficient sleep is for the consolidation of what you have learned. A study from 2014 showed that students who slept more than the comparison group performed significantly better. In another study, these positive effects were even proven in babies between four and sixteen months old.

The opposite was also investigated: how does lack of sleep affect mental performance and thus learning? Anyone who sleeps less than six hours over two weeks is then as mentally restricted as someone who has not slept for forty-eight hours! And the mental abilities of someone who has received less than four hours of sleep over the course of five nights are similar to those of a drunk! This is particularly frightening because, at least until recently, some industries considered it a kind of professional distinction to work harder and sleep less. Also, students often enough make the mistake of pulling all-nighters, working through the night with very little sleep to cram before an exam. Little of what they are trying to memorise will actually stick in their brains, not even in the short term, and this is exacerbated by the lack of sleep which makes it an even more futile effort.

Interestingly, it seems that it is not only the type of sleep that determines whether or not a certain learning material is consolidated in the memory, but also whether the brain thinks that the material is important or not. In a study carried out in 2010, volunteers were given material to learn but not told that they would still need it the next day. Both groups had the same amount of study time and sleep. Those who had not been told that they would be tested on the material the next day scored way worse on the test the following morning than those who had been told. Our brain seems to consolidate only what is recognized as important and transfers the information into long-term memory during sleep. Therefore, it can be worthwhile to go through the learned contents again before going to sleep to underline its importance.

From all of this, some clear recommendations regarding your sleeping habits will emerge:

1. Ensure adequate and undisturbed sleep

Only if you sleep enough will you help your brain consolidate what you have learned during the day. How much is enough will depend on you, but a general rule is that you should get at least seven and a half hours of undisturbed sleep.

It is also important that your sleep is undisturbed by distracting sounds or lights. It is true that there are people who have become so used to sleeping with a certain level of light that for them sleeping in a completely dark room feels too uncomfortable or even scary and they cannot do it anymore. But if you can, get rid of any light sources during the night, including little LED lights on TVs or the time display on an alarm clock. These all keep you from getting the deep sleep you deserve.

2. Sleep regularly

If you go to bed and get up at the same time regularly, your body will get used to these times and will almost automatically become tired at the usual time in the evening and will be awake and fresh in the morning when you get up. This may not always be possible in normal everyday life, but if you want to support your mental capacity in general and your learning ability in particular, you should keep the exceptions as limited as possible. This regularity enables your body to sleep more deeply and your sleep will be more restful, especially as the deep sleep phases are very important for consolidating what you have learned during the day.

3. Create a sleep ritual

On nights when you go to bed at your usual time, you could get into the habit of doing certain things regularly to support your undisturbed sleep.

In the hour before you go to bed, try to avoid all excitement and stress if possible. This includes action movies, thrillers, or highly emotional films.

Smartphones, computers and tablets should not be used during this time as the blue light reduces the production of the sleep hormone melatonin and you will get tired less quickly. Functions like Nightshift on smartphones can reduce this effect but cannot completely prevent it.

Since the brain concentrates on storing important information in the long-term memory during sleep, you could go through the day's learning content right before falling asleep. If you take the notes with you to bed, read them and go through them again in your mind, your brain will know that all these things are important. If you then also recall your learning goal and your motivation to learn, you can fall asleep knowing that you have given your brain an explicit order for the night.

So in the end, it *is* possible to learn in your sleep!

Stress

There are many factors that influence your learning success, and stress is certainly one of the main ones. That which is often referred to as stress and which today has such a negative connotation has been an essential mechanism for the survival of the human race during human development. When man was still living in caves and survival was at stake daily in any situation of imminent danger, non-essential functions of the body were shut down, including digestion and sex drive; other functions such as pulse and respiration were increased, allowing for greater physical performance. In this way, the ability to survive either by fight or flight was significantly increased. When the acute danger was over, the body functions returned to their previous balanced state.

This mechanism is controlled by certain hormones in the body, which are released when needed and cause certain physical reactions. Cortisol is the most important stress hormone. If a person gets into a stressful situation, more cortisol is released, causing the heart rate to increase and more energy in the form of blood sugars to be available for strength and endurance

However, the stress of which we usually speak today has very little to do with the original function of ensuring survival. The situations that cause us stress today are not about our survival, but more often about socially stressful situations such as a presentation in front of other people, the fear of not being able to meet a deadline or other negative social interactions. It is always about uncertainty, unpredictability and the threat to status and reputation.

The causes of this type of stress very often do not just last a few minutes or hours, but for many people they will last for weeks, months or even years. This type of permanent stress means that the body does not sufficiently return to its normal balanced state and thus runs the risk of permanent damage. That means that good stress management in general is very important for us humans in today's world.

Many learning situations are also associated with stress—the preparation of tests and exams under time pressure, especially an oral exam—where the fear of presenting in front of other people is often added to the pressure to perform.

Learning stress of any kind, whether acute exam stress or continuous stress, means that the high level of cortisol in the brain leads to changes that make learning difficult. High levels of cortisol mean that the connections between the nerve cells in the brain (the neurons) are reduced, which slows down data transmission at the synapses, i.e. the interfaces between the nerve cells.

What normally happens during learning is the exact opposite: the synaptic connections are strengthened and thus the speed of data transmission between neurons is increased. When information is retrieved, for example, during an oral examination or a written test, cortisol can impede this process and thus slow down the brain's ability to retrieve previously stored information.

What, then, are some helpful strategies to counteract the negative effects of stress on learning?

Observe your general stress levels

If you learn to check your level of stress regularly, you can take countermeasures and find ways to relax. Not only will this be generally healthier for you, it also helps you to improve your general ability to learn.

One way to relax even during an intensive learning phase is to gauge how far you have progressed with your learning and what you have learned compared to two or even four weeks ago. By looking at your successes, you gain new motivation and increase your faith in yourself with the certainty that you *can* do it!

Of course, stress management techniques such as autogenic training, progressive muscle relaxation or breathing techniques can also help.

Get moving

As we have seen, regular exercise not only helps you to be fitter and healthier, but also to reduce stress. Any type of movement will do; just going for a walk for half an hour every day can already make a big difference.

Use rituals before learning

I have found it helpful to follow a certain ritual before each learning unit. For me, it does not only consist of reminding me of my motivation to learn as described in the section above, but also of taking a few deep breaths and doing some relaxation exercises. This helps, especially when the daily routine before and after learning is quite hectic. I try to relax and be less stressed during my study time.

Find a quiet place to study

The more you reduce distractions while you learn, the greater the chance that you can relax a little while learning. Avoid unnecessary ambient noises, especially those that are very irregular and loud.

I am often asked if listening to music is distracting to someone who is learning. This one is a very personal decision, but it also depends on the type of music in general. If you find that music helps you because it relaxes you, then listen to your favourite music but rather quietly in the background. If it is played too loud, it is likely to distract you too much. Also make sure that the music triggers positive feelings and does not make you feel sad or aggressive. Music that makes you happy and is not too restless will help if it relaxes you.

Warm up your brain before learning

Just like in sports, it is beneficial to warm up before intensive training or learning units. If you play a musical instrument, do so a few minutes right before learning; this way, you prepare your brain for the coming unit by increasing your concentration and creativity. Because you need both of these things to learn, this is a pleasant way to get into the right state!

Summary

How you treat your body does not only have an influence on your health, it can also help or hinder your memory. The better you look after your body with the right food, sufficient water, regular exercise and adequate sleep, the better your brain will be at learning and storing information. This makes a difference even when you apply all the techniques in this book since you still have to learn your memory pictures and stories.

Review questions

1. How often a week should you do some kind of exercise to help your brain function better?
2. Why does moving your body while you are learning make it even more effective?
3. What are foods that help your brain function better?
4. Which ones do you already consume regularly?
5. What are the negative effects of lack of sleep?
6. Why is it so important to sleep regularly and sufficiently?
7. What can you do to reduce your stress levels?
8. How can you use music to help you learn better?

Implementation

1. Schedule exercise into your calendar or start a daily 7-minute routine.
2. Go through the list of brain foods and choose a few you can easily add to your daily diet, either in your meals or as healthy snacks in between. If this replaces unhealthy snacks such as crisps, regular chocolate or other snacks high in sugar, this might even help you lose weight!
3. Look at your stress level and follow the tips mentioned above. Just a minor change in your routine can have a tremendous long-term effect!

CHAPTER 8

GOING FORWARD

Wow! Congratulations on having successfully completed the book! I am really proud of you and really happy that you went through the entire book. I hope you did not only read through it but also did all of the exercises. Did you?

The big question for you now is: how much have you been able to improve your memory? Let us find out. Here is the test you did in the beginning in the same format with adjusted content, so it is comparable to the entry test. Do the test now, write down your results at the end and compare them to your initial results. Depending on how you did in the beginning and how much you have practised, I would expect you to see an improvement of thirty to sixty points.

Before you do the test, I have a few ideas on how you can really make all you have learnt here stick and maximise its impact on your own development, and become a master of the art of learning.

Make a concrete plan

In his book about the principles of the most successful people, Napoleon Hill wrote: "Plan your work and work your plan." This also applies to you if you wish to make the most out of your new memory powers. Since you have made it this far, there are surely areas in your professional or personal life where you need to acquire new knowledge or skills. Write down what they are, create a document with all the details you wish to learn and then make a learning plan, including your optimal repetitions from Chapter 2. Schedule your specific learning sessions so you block the time to do them. Then start implementing your plan.

In the beginning, the various standard lists you have learned may not yet be safely anchored in your brain. It would then be helpful to select the standard list you want to use on a specific topic and alternate between lists. This helps to avoid what I call picture overlap on the one hand and serves as extra practice to repeat your standard lists.

It also helps to read through your plan every morning. I have scheduled this in my calendar as well because I have found this to be vital for implementing my plan.

Dedicate time to practise

As Tony Robbins always says: "Repetition is the mother of skill." There is no mastery without regular practice. Tiger Woods, one of the greatest golfers of all time, does not simply go home after a day at a tournament. He is said to go to the putting green and keep putting until he has sunk a hundred balls in a row. Dirk Nowitzki, of Dallas Mavericks fame and the sixth best scorer in basketball history, practises throwing the ball after matches when his teammates have already gone home.

Now you have learnt how the memory techniques work. You know the theory and have practised with a few examples. But this does not mean that you have mastered the art of learning fully yet! To make it a powerful skill and habit, I recommend you dedicate at least half an hour every day to practising for the next thirty days. Learn a few names, new vocabulary, a thirty- or fifty-digit number and a list of facts every day to get your brain into the habit. If you do this for a month, you will start reaping the full benefits of these techniques.

Look for application possibilities

Another way to train your memory is to look for application possibilities in your everyday work life. Ask yourself: "Where could additional knowledge help me professionally?" Once you start asking this question regularly, you will very soon start seeing more opportunities for learning to advance your career. Your mind will continuously be on the lookout for ways to advance your career through targeted learning. Now that you know how to learn faster, you also have the confidence that you can implement it.

Gather the materials, include them in your learning plan and then start learning systematically, even if it is for only twenty minutes every day. Once you start doing this, within a few weeks you should start seeing positive changes in how you behave at your job: with more competence, with more confidence and with more credibility!

Cross off your to-dos

Whenever I have finished a task that I had planned to do, I like to cross it off my list. And I literally mean to cross it off. I take a pen and put a big cross through the entry on my to-do list for that day. This is only possible when you have a physical plan in the form of a sheet of paper. In case I have written it on my computer or phone, I also delete the entry. It might not have as strong of an effect as when I take a pen and cross a to-do off of the paper list, but it still feels good.

When you do this, you officially "finish the to-do" and this act will give you a motivation boost by releasing dopamine, the reward hormone, into your bloodstream. This gives you a feeling of satisfaction and with that, the energy to get the next task done.

Review your progress

Every now and again, it helps to look at where you stand and compare it to where you were last week or last month. This can be in terms of the things you have successfully memorised or the progress you have made in applying the memory techniques. This review will show you how much more powerful your memory has become and provide further motivation to keep you on track to becoming a memory superstar!

No more notes

Next time you give a presentation or deliver a speech, learn the content upfront and deliver your presentation without ever consulting the slides or any written notes. This will be far more impressive than reading off of the slides or continuously looking at a sheet of paper. Instead, keep eye contact with your audience at all times and connect with them. This will leave a much stronger impression on your listeners and help you establish your credibility as an expert.

Observe your thinking

I mentioned in the introduction that there is a positive side effect to using these picture-based memory techniques. Since your brain will constantly look for ways to connect even the most unrelated things, it will develop more net-worked thinking. That means you should notice after a while that you will start having more associations in everyday situations. You will connect ideas more easily and automatically and, in this way, become more creative.

Another positive side effect is an increase in self-confidence. When you keep experiencing that you can learn, store and recall information much faster than before, easier than ever and for longer periods of time, your belief in your ability to master future challenges will increase over time. This might lead you to overcome more challenges, seize more opportunities, and in the end become more successful in life. Keep observing how you think and behave so you can notice any positive changes and consciously build on them.

Teach others and spread the news

I am happy for any progress that you have made and will be making. I would be even happier if you could help others have the same opportunity. Show your family and friends what you are able to do now, how you do it, and maybe give them a copy of this book as a gift so they can study the techniques as well. Also, share your experiences on social media so others will learn about the possibilities that a trained memory can give them.

TEST YOUR MEMORY

How does the test work?

This exit test works the same way as the initial test. Take a pen, some paper and a timer (perhaps on your mobile phone) and sit down in a quiet place where you will not be disturbed.

Read the instructions carefully before each exercise. As soon as you have finished, set the timer to the specified time. Once it starts, memorise as much of the information as possible. When the timer has finished, count backwards in increments of 7 from 100, i.e. 100, 93, 86, etc. When you get to 2, write down all the things you recall from the exercise and then check how many of them you got right.

When you have done all the exercises, add up your points for your overall score. Write down your results in the table at the end of the test or on a sheet of paper. When you have finished the test, compare your results to the results of the initial test. Where did you improve the most? Where might you benefit from more practice?

I. Shopping list

Duration: 1 minute; maximum score: 20

Remember as many of the things on this shopping list as possible. For each correct item you get one point, another one for the correct position on the list.

1. butter
2. almonds
3. cheese
4. bananas
5. bread roll
6. chips
7. screws
8. lavender
9. guitar strings
10. travel guide

II. Abstract words

Duration: 3 minutes; maximum score: 40

Learn the following twenty words in the order given. For each correct word, you get one point. For the correct position on the list, you get another point.

1. trumpet
2. to jump
3. noise
4. birth
5. cleanliness
6. briefly
7. spontaneous
8. mould
9. alternating current
10. impatient
11. nuclear power
12. rescue
13. laboratory test
14. science
15. attentive
16. homework
17. heat
18. race
19. wind
20. university

III. Telephone numbers

Duration: 3 minutes; maximum score: 30

This part is about learning different phone numbers. For each correct number, you get five points. When you allocate it to the correct person, you get another point.

1. Uncle Mark: 4578349
2. Grandpa: 787 3927368
3. Mrs Schultheis: 249736
4. Justin Bellheim: 97531987
5. Grocery store: 8345804

IV. Vocabulary

Duration: 3 minutes; maximum score: 30

Learn the following fantasy words. For each correct translation, you get three points if the spelling is correct. For each letter spelled incorrectly, there is a one-point deduction per word.

TV - vrellma
bicycle - falmaka
music - tellibra
sun - snegging
fence - daufall
sand - managol
painting - ritting
lamp - schneiso
mouse - lanfata
guitar - schwonk

V. Faces and names

Duration: 2 minutes; maximum score: 40

Learn the first and last names of the following people and their faces. For each correctly remembered first name and surname, you get two points; for each name you match to the correct face, you get one point. For each misspelled letter, there is a one-point deduction for that name.

Jeremy Shaw

Alice Griffith

Dominic Cook

Jack Bennett

Hailey Smith

Max Richards

Jenny Black

Dane Price

VI. Task list

Duration: 2 minutes; maximum score: 20

Memorise the following ten tasks. Again, there is one point given for each correctly remembered task and another one for the correct position on the list.

1. Walk the dog
2. Order monitor cable
3. Empty dustbin
4. Bake a cake
5. Collect parcel from your neighbour
6. Guitar practice
7. Write a letter to mother
8. Go jogging
9. Water flowers
10. Take a nap

VII. Facts about Steve Jobs

Duration: 1.5 minutes; maximum score: 20

Here are some interesting facts about Steve Jobs. For each correctly remembered fact, independent of the order, you get two points.

1. Born in 1955
2. Birthplace San Francisco
3. Founder of Apple and Pixar Animation Studios
4. Was temporarily a fruitarian
5. Assets in 2011 8.3 billion US dollars according to Forbes Magazine
6. Daughter Lisa
7. Famous speech at Stanford University
8. Friend of Bill Gates
9. Annual salary 1 US Dollar
10. Died in 2011

Review

I. Shopping list

For each correct item you get one point, another one for the correct position on the list.

1. _____

2. _____

3. _____

4. _____

5. _____

6. _____

7. _____

8. _____

9. _____

10. _____

Number of points: _____

II. Abstract words

For each correct word, you get one point. For the correct position on the list, you get another point.

1. _____

2. _____

3. _____

4. _____

5. _____

6. _____

7. _____

8. _____

9. _____

10. _____

11. _____

12. _____

13. _____

14. _____

15. _____

16. _____

17. _____

18. _____

19. _____

20. _____

Number of points: _____

III. Telephone numbers

For each correct number, you get five points. When you allocate it to the correct person, you get another point.

1. Mrs Schultheis: _____

2. Uncle Mark: _____

3. Justin Bellheim: _____

4. Grocery store: _____

5. Grandpa: _____

Number of points: _____

IV. Vocabulary

For each correct translation, you get three points if the spelling is correct. For each letter spelled incorrectly, there is a one-point deduction per word.

TV - _____

bicycle - _____

_____ - tellibra

sun - _____

_____ - daufall

sand - _____

_____ - ritting

lamp - _____

_____ - lanfata

_____ - schwonk

Number of points: _____

V. Faces and names

For each correctly remembered first name and surname, you get two points; for each name you match to the correct face, you get one point. For each misspelled letter, there is a one-point deduction for that name.

_____ _____ _____ _____

_____ _____ _____ _____

Number of points: _____

VI. Task list

You get one point for each correctly remembered task and another one for the correct position on the list.

1. _____

2. _____

3. _____

4. _____

5. _____

6. _____

7. _____

8. _____

9. _____

10. _____

Number of points: _____

VII. Facts about Steve Jobs

For each correctly remembered fact, independent of the order, you get two points.

1. _____

2. _____

3. _____

4. _____

5. _____

6. _____

7. _____

8. _____

9. _____

10. _____

Number of points: _____

Overall result

I.	Shopping list	_____points
II.	Abstract words	_____points
III.	Telephone numbers	_____points
IV.	Vocabulary	_____points
V.	Faces and names	_____points
VI.	Task list	_____points
VII.	Facts about Steve Jobs	_____points

TOTAL NUMBER OF POINTS: _____ **out of 200 possible points**

BIBLIOGRAPHY

Robbins, Anthony. 1986. *Unlimited Power.* New York: Simon & Schuster.

Canfield, Jack. 2005. *The Success Principles.* New York: HarperCollins.

Coyle, Daniel. 2009. *The Talent Code.* London: Penguin Random House.

Spantidi, Maria. 2020. *Fluent for Free.*

Graves, Grant. 2020. *Fearless.*

Hill, Napoleon. 2003. *Think and Grow Rich.* Penguin Group

Keller, Gary. 2014. *The ONE Thing.* London: Bard Press

ACKNOWLEDGMENTS

I would like to thank the following people without whom this book would never have seen the light of day:

- My loving wife Sabine for all her support, especially in the late phases before getting this book to the market.

- My son Paul for his willingness to learn and for his creativity in coming up with memory pictures.

- My son Johann for loving me the way that I am.

- My parents: my father for instilling in me a deep desire for and interest in learning; my mother for implanting the belief in me that I can achieve anything.

- My brothers for always being there for me when I really needed them.

- My teacher Mrs. Tiedemann for teaching me how to work in a very structured way.

- My friend Jennifer for her inspiration to just read up on any interesting topic.

- My friend Iris for helping me refine the tests.

- My coach Roel for accompanying me for all these years and helping me find my vocation.

- My coach Gary at self-publishingschool.com for all your great advice.

- My editor Sandi for all the extremely helpful comments.

- The people at 100covers.com and formattedbooks.com for really getting the book into shape.

My launch team for all your valuable advice and support in the launch phase of the book.

Last, but certainly not least, you, my reader, for your interest in the book and for implementing the techniques in your life.

ABOUT THE AUTHOR

Peter Szczensny is an international memory trainer who has trained and coached people in German and English on how to master the art of learning. His students include people of all ages, from primary school children to adults to the elderly.

As a child and teenager, he grew up in a household where education and learning played an important role and where learning was made easy. Here Peter picked up various skills in sports, music, organisation and leadership and experienced the value of learning firsthand.

During his professional career, he held various leadership positions in international companies helped by his ability to acquire new knowledge fast. To this day, he continues to develop his professional knowledge and skills in such areas as leadership, personal development and project management.

He lives with his wife and two sons in Mönchengladbach, Germany.

CAN YOU HELP?

Thank You for Reading My Book!

I really appreciate all of your feedback, and I
love hearing what you have to say.

I need your input to make the next version of
this book and my future books better.

Please leave me a helpful review on Amazon letting me know what
you thought of the book. To access the review page, just go to review.
masteroflearning.com and you will be redirected automatically.

Also, if you liked what you have learnt from this book, please share it
on your favourite social media sites like Facebook, Twitter or Instagram.
Tell all your friends, family members and colleagues about it.

Thank you very much in advance!

Peter Szczensny

Made in the USA
Middletown, DE
20 October 2021

50697135R00096